DATE DUE

OE 10 '96			
NE 19 '97			
OE 18 '98			
DE 21 '02			
JE 5 '03			

DEMCO 38-296

CONFRONTING
DIVERSITY
ISSUES
ON CAMPUS

S U R V I V A L   S K I L L S   F O R   S C H O L A R S

Managing Editor: Mitchell Allen

Survival Skills for Scholars provides you, the professor or advanced graduate student working in a college or university setting, with practical suggestions for making the most of your academic career. These brief, readable guides will help you with skills that you are required to master as a college professor but may have never been taught in graduate school. Using hands-on, jargon-free advice and examples, forms, lists, and suggestions for additional resources, experts on different aspects of academic life give invaluable tips on managing the day-to-day tasks of academia—effectively and efficiently.

Volumes in This Series

CONFRONTING DIVERSITY ISSUES ON CAMPUS

BENJAMIN P. BOWSER

GALE S. AULETTA

TERRY JONES

SAGE Publications
International Educational and Professional Publisher
Newbury Park   London   New Delhi

For information address:

SAGE Publications, Inc.
2455 Teller Road
Newbury Park, California 91320

SAGE Publications Ltd.
6 Bonhill Street
London EC2A 4PU
United Kingdom

SAGE Publications India Pvt. Ltd.
M-32 Market
Greater Kailash I
New Delhi 110 048 India

Printed in the United States of America

Library of Congress Cataloging-in-Publication Data

Bowser, Benjamin P.
    Confronting diversity issues on campus / Benjamin P. Bowser,
        Gale S. Auletta, Terry Jones
        p. cm. — (Survival skills for scholars ; vol. 6)
    Includes bibliographical references.
    ISBN 0-8039-5215-5 — ISBN 0-8039-5216-3 (pbk.)
    1. Multicultural education—United States. 2. Minorities—
Education (Higher)—United States. 3. College teachers—United
States—Attitudes. 4. College teaching—United States.
I. Auletta, Gale S. II. Jones, Terry. III. Title. IV. Series.
LC1099.3.B69 1993
370.19′6—dc20   93-5199
                                                                    CIP

93 94 95 96 10 9 8 7 6 5 4 3 2 1

Sage Production Editor: Yvonne Könneker

Contents

This book is dedicated to all the faculty, students, staff members, and administrators of all points of view who have over the years shared with us their stories, hopes, fears, frustrations, rages, mistakes, and successes. Thank you for being in the struggle. You inspire and motivate us.

Preface*

When our editor, Mitch Allen, first asked us to write what we interpreted to be a book on "Everything you wanted to know about diversity, but were afraid to ask" in 100 pages or fewer, we laughed. It could not be done, even if it came in the mail wrapped in a brown paper bag. It would simplify complex issues that are already being maligned as insignificant, nonacademic, propagandistic, and trendy. We have each devoted 20 years or more to studying, teaching, and writing on these issues. How could we do the topic justice in 100 pages?

Well, thanks to Mitch Allen's persuasive ability, our joy in working with one another, and the fact that we are daredevils at heart, we accepted this challenge.

We accepted because we are saddened, angered, and frustrated by what we see and hear as the growing racial divide in higher education. We hear our well-meaning European-American faculty colleagues in many institutions all across the country ignore or downplay the importance of the racial experiences of faculty members and students of color. We feel their nervousness and discomfort when they talk about race relations. We are embarrassed for them when their guilt and ignorance means they made "bad affirmative action hires."

*This book is equally coauthored by all three authors. The order of the names was arbitrarily established.

We know they care. Yet we also hurt when the students and faculty of color tell us: "That professor singles me out because I'm African-American"; "That professor is not calling on me because he thinks that because I am Vietnamese that he won't be able to understand me"; or "Here I go again—the only professor of color in the department. I wonder if I am the token?"

We empathize with and are enraged by faculty members who do not acknowledge the existence of the racial divide. To ignore, argue, or rationalize away the racial and gender differences breeds a hostility and withdrawal so intense that it is difficult for any student learning to occur or for any faculty of color to feel loyalty for our colleges. Yet many faculty members fear that to confront the differences will unleash and ignite the rage and frustrations and increase the racial divide.

We believe that being aware of the racial divide and of the vast differences between us creates the space for the shared meanings and connections to evolve. Because we believe in this paradox so strongly, we accepted Mitch's challenge, given that we could expose the wounds of diversity. This handbook spotlights the ways in which our academic culture and we, as academics, contribute daily to the racial wounds that divide. We also offer "doable" strategies that can promote a more healing and inclusive institution.

To undertake a book about diversity and teaching strategies in higher education is to move out of the safe harbor of tradition and over the deep, uncharted waters where the wind roars and the billows roll. However, in these uncharted waters there are opportunities to explore and new energies to harness and utilize.

The Authors: Who Are We?

Yes, we participated in the conflicts of the 1960s. And yes, we are card-carrying activists. We were among the influx of "new students"—that is, African-Americans, Native Americans, Latinos and Latinas, Asian-Americans, and women of all ethnicities. We confronted the power structure and demanded change. We questioned what was being taught, who was doing the teaching, and how they were teaching. Along with thousands of students across the country, we asked the questions that focused attention on the traditions of higher education and its basic underpinnings. These challenges and questions have not destroyed higher education. To the contrary, we believe that they have both worked to elevate standards and move it in the direction of greater inclusiveness.

We are now tenured and successful—and some say radical—professors who are passionately loyal to the institution of higher education and want it to be more inclusive. We are two African-American males and one European-American female who, despite our academic standings, have experienced the pain and punishment of oppression in our lives.

We are teachers. Benjamin Bowser, a sociologist, teaches graduate and undergraduate courses in research methods and the sociology of minority groups. Terry Jones, also a sociologist as well as a social worker, teaches the sociology of minority groups and African-American family courses. Gale Auletta, a communications professor, teaches courses in intercultural and interpersonal communication.

Among us we have more than 60 years of experience studying, writing, doing research, consulting, leading workshops, administering departments and programs and getting grants, observing, interviewing, traveling, and devoting most of our time thinking about how racial and cultural relations could be improved in the United States. Although we have long professional resumes and have published, what is more important for this book, we believe, is our years of personal experience living with what we study. We have made our mistakes and have had our successes; along the way we have angered and agitated more than a few and have been honestly challenged by many. We feel great empathy for all who care enough to make mistakes, learn, change, and go on to make new mistakes and learn and change again.

We may write some things that will make you uncomfortable, even angry. That is the nature of the topic. What we do hope to do is engage you to think and try to implement some of our ideas. If we are really successful, you will experiment with and write about other ways of knowing and behaving in the multicultural university.

We Have an Attitude

We believe that in a race-conscious society, race, racism, and other ways to oppress people of color take primacy in framing discussions about diversity and the multicultural perspective. People of color, especially Native Americans, African-Americans, Latinos and Latinas, and Asian-Americans have been peculiarly abused in this society. Not paying particular homage to this fact reduces the multicultural analysis to little more than a guided tour: "Here is what the Indians do on Christmas day. Now let's take a look at the Chinese—and oh, aren't those Japanese good with mathematics. Tell us what we need to know about the Cambodians." That is not what we have to offer here.

Racism is three things: (a) a cultural presumption in one race's superiority and another's inferiority; (b) institutional practices that reinforce and fulfill the cultural presumption; and (c) individual beliefs in the racist cultural presumption and institutional practices. Moreover, we believe that racism as it is practiced in the United States is primarily the responsibility of European-Americans to solve. Our experience has taught us that even though African-Americans, Latinos and Latinas, Native Americans, and Asian-Americans may have the ability to practice individual racism, they rarely have the power or position to engage in institutionalized racism or to change the culture.

We urge you not to be turned off by the word *racism*. We know that racism is an action word: It incites. It tenses up an otherwise peaceful situation; it immobilizes some and emboldens others. That is why understanding racism and its pervasiveness are major themes in this book. We live in a society that wants to both exploit and deny the pervasiveness of racism, so to not address racism would be a disservice to you and the issue. Yet before you decide that this is just another diatribe on racism, we urge you to read a little further because what we hope to do is to model for you ways to discuss racism in mixed company.

Discussions on diversity have thus far tended to blend and push to the background the institutional and structural issues that create exclusion based on race, gender, or physical ability. We are concerned that our colleagues all across the country appear to feel freer and more willing to discuss diversity and multicultural education if racism is omitted from the topic. Moreover, we believe if we can confront racism in diversity the other hurdles will be much lower.

So, our focus is on race and cultural differences in the academy and the differences they make. We know that gender, class, physical abilities, and sexual orientation differences also matter tremendously, but we will not focus on these other issues. We believe that the themes we present (not the particulars) also apply to these other forms of exclusion.

This book looks at how people interact with one another in interracial and unequal power relationships. We spotlight the internal racial conflicts that people carry with them to the learning place that either enhance or detract from the educational process. For example, does an African-American student feel that she is "selling out" by attending a "white" university? Do feelings of mistrust that a Mexican-American student has for European-Americans create such anxiety that it is difficult to concentrate on studies? What happens when the European-American male professor's beliefs in the universality of the Eurocentric perspective make him anxious and hostile when Asian students complain that there is no mention of China in a world history course? There is a special burden that accompanies people when they invade traditionally all European-American institutions. The invaders are seen by some as tokens, sometimes as affirmative action hires, and sometimes even as threats to the academic integrity of the institution. They are seen by others as the proverbial missing link to quality higher education. We try to personalize the impact that our cultural burdens and baggage have on others: the confusion, anger, misunderstandings, frustration, and withdrawal.

In addition, we believe that we are all in the college context but in different ways—and these different experiences matter. We contend that the policies, curricula, teaching methods, distribution of scarce resources, race and gender of those who hold power, and the history of relationships all influence the type and quality of experience that people from diverse backgrounds have in college. Universities that have virtually all European-American administrators and a mostly European-American male faculty and are all Eurocentric in perspective will see it as normal to have people of color and women as peripheral to the whole. Such institutions are not responding effectively to the future and to the challenge of cultural and racial diversity.

We know that most faculty members, administrators, and students of all colors are fair-minded good people who want to understand better how to improve their relationships with students of other races and cultures. There are tremendous personal and professional benefits to making such an effort. Ignorance, prejudice, discrimination, and racism are hurtful to the whole of society, not just to people of color and women. Left unchecked, these negative qualities work to create a false sense of superiority in European-Americans and a false sense of inferiority in people of color. As the university student community begins to more accurately reflect the diversity of people in this nation and in the world community, it is imperative that we focus on overcoming those issues that exclude and denigrate.

The Format of This Book

We draw from a rich variety of research and theory that is referenced for you at the end of the book. However, this is not intended to be an exhaustive and definitive literature review. It is more of a quick guide, a bag of strategies and suggestions that can be used to engage others in cooperative dialogue and inclusive action. Our objective is to focus on principles, to model opening discussions on a variety of key topics and to arm European-American and faculty members of color alike with some basic instruments for navigating in the multicultural college community. We cannot possibly write about every possible diversity group, but we do provide a paradigm for raising questions that allows the reader to generate the means for pursuing his or her own avenues. We offer you nothing that will make you politically correct. We rely on mini-case studies, sample interactions, and diversity stories to set the stage or to exemplify important points in the chapters. These examples are real. We have personally witnessed or heard firsthand reports from others. Only the names have been changed.

Although you may not have experienced any of these actual situations, please know that our research and our experiences on campuses all across the country suggest that the true stories we tell are representative. We encourage you to think of the variations that apply to your own circumstances.

A Word About Labels

Grouping individuals and placing them under one cultural or ethnic or racial label is dangerous and often false. But it is also sometimes necessary. With that said, how did we choose the labels we used? Carefully, contradictorily, and arbitrarily. While one of the tenets of this book is that how others perceive our physical and color attributes matters, we still wanted to move away from color-coded terms. *Black* and *white* are often-heard terms, but *brown*, *red*, and *yellow* are not as common. We felt the need to be consistent and contemporary but, more important, we wanted to move away from such simplistic, culturally void terms. However, when referring to all of the groups in the United States that do not "look like" and are oppressed by the dominant European-Americans, we use the term *people of color* to emphasize that the United States and its colleges and universities are still stratified by color. In all other cases, we refer to groups by their more precise culture terms as hyphenated Americans: European-, Asian-, African-, Latin, and Native Americans. Our intent here is to represent the multicultured character of the United States more accurately. With the exception of Native Americans and indigenous Latinos and Latinas, we are a nation of people who came from someplace else as immigrants, refugees, or slaves.

We are not completely comfortable with using hyphenated American labels. They are also general and ethnocentric. We need terms that more precisely denote our presence in the United States rather than assuming the American continent as our own. We strongly suggest that whenever speaking to a particular cultural group or an individual whose ethnic identity is known to be different from yours, that you ask and refer to that group or individual by whatever ethnic or racial term is preferred by them.

The Chapters in This Book

Chapter 1, "The Unwritten Organization," exposes several unwritten and informal rules that can become traps and pitfalls for the unknowing, especially people of color. "What you see is not what you necessarily get." There is no place where this saying is truer than in higher education. The rules may say one thing, but the informal culture often says another. The promotion, retention, and tenure documents state that you must publish, but the committee says you must publish in the "right" journals. This chapter views the murky underground of the informal structure of the university through the eyes of faculty members and students of color and offers some suggestions for survival.

Chapter 2, "What Did You Say You Were? Am I a Racist?" is a straightforward discussion of racial identity and the myths and realities of racism as we know them in the United States. The chapter focuses on commonly held beliefs that many of us hold about race and provides a look at the realities obscured by these myths. This knowledge is absolutely essential to better communications, the resolution of personal and institutional conflict, and growth that is both personal and professional, as you will see in subsequent chapters.

Chapter 3, "Communication, Communication, Communication!" highlights the importance of our daily communication about diversity. All too often in academia we emphasize the content and harm the relationship between teacher and student or between colleagues. We provide a set of dividers and connectors for understanding how the same content can be stated to support and confirm the relationship or can be phrased in such a way as to estrange the relationship. The dividers contribute to a hostile racial environment, and the connectors demonstrate ways of being more sensitive and inclusive when talking about potentially divisive issues in interracial interactions.

Chapter 4, "Dealing With Conflict and Diversity in the Academic Community," unpacks four major and inevitable conflicts that arise when cultures collide in college environments. We tackle four of the biggies: (a) the purpose of education, (b) affirmative action, (c) freedom of speech, and (d) the role of ethnic studies. The concepts developed in the preceding chapters are used to analyze the conflicts. In addition, we suggest possible resolution strategies and their consequences.

In Chapter 5, "Toward New Racial and Cultural Boundaries in the Academy," we talk about *communities of interest* and the necessity of redefining them. How do the many cultural and ethnic groups within the university nurture and support their own concerns while also contributing to a more inclusive definition of the college community? Moreover, we summarize the earlier chapters by way of suggesting "doable" strategies for both individuals and institutions. We provide models of people who have been successful in grounding their personal identities in nonracist soil and have bridged the racial and cultural barriers.

Now, sit back, relax, and enjoy living the questions and the dilemmas that this little book presents.

1 | The Unwritten Organization

A colleague described the experience of being a professional of color in higher education as like being in an amusement park. You enter a room with mirrors that give you the illusion that the floor is level. But when you walk, it is obviously tilted. What is maddening is that when you ask others if they feel the tilted floor, they look at you like you are crazy and suggest that you are either too sensitive or unhappy here and should go elsewhere.

Why would this colleague perceive higher education as being so tilted and inequitable when so many of us believe that academia is the most fair and equitable of all social institutions? The fact is that both his and our perceptions are correct. The explanation for the apparent contradiction is quite simple. Universities and colleges as formal organizations and in outward appearances look like fair and equitable organizations. If you look no further, then our colleague's perception does suggest a talent for fiction. But if we look at universities and colleges as informal organizations with unwritten institutional cultures and practices, then our colleague is correct. What goes on beneath and behind the formal, corporate, professed, and written organization? It is where actions are taken or not taken to produce inequities in the use of resources, participation, and influence by race. Through the informal life of an institution, one can maintain historic racial and cultural privileges while professing and giving the appearance of fairness.

How could such sleight of hand be possible? The answer can be given by anyone who has directed a program, chaired a department, been on the tenure track, or managed an office. There are the rules, and then there is the way things get done: practice, the informal "rules," and institutional culture. The rules and actual practices are not mutually exclusive, but there is overlap. University and college communities reflect this reality. In fact, relatively few of the rules and practices that define a tradition-laden institution such as the university or an academic department are formally spelled out.

The university system of governance is based on an informal and covert way of doing things that continues to control the extent to which racial and non-European cultural groups participate in American institutional life. In the past, one particular ethnic or racial group might have overtly monopolized positions of power and privilege in an institution. But now a similar monopoly can be established covertly by defining and monopolizing the institution's informal life. This is not necessarily a conscious act. More often it is the consequence of the historically privileged (not all European-Americans, by any means) not examining their traditional practices, assuming that the university or department is theirs and that minority students, faculty members, or administrators of color are outsiders. If you feel that an institution belongs to you, then you should control it and have the right to determine who will belong. Two real-world cases will illustrate this point.

The Unwritten Rules

In the first case, we will see how the unwritten rules can be used to meaningfully increase the numbers of successful students of color in a graduate department. (See Chart 1.1.)

Chart 1.1 The Unwritten Rules

1. The university is political.
2. Personal and professional networks are powerful forces.
3. People of color are perceived as threats.
4. Hidden agendas vary in sophistication.
5. Hidden agendas cannot tolerate public exposure.
6. Perceptions matter.

Case 1: Using the Unwritten Rules

Professor William G., a European-American, and several departmental colleagues at an Ivy League university decided to recruit, enroll, and train several students of color in their field each year. The department did not initially have the applicants or money to support them. The department members first identified prospective applicants of color through colleagues at other universities. Next, they struck a deal with their dean to get recruitment money and several assistantships each year. Then they got several very talented students of color to apply, many of whom did not meet the mandatory grade-point-average (GPA) requirements. The graduate school admitted the students on a provisional and trial basis. Once the students were enrolled, Bill G. and his colleagues provided regular counseling and mentoring. The students did well and have graduated and moved on to distinguish themselves in their profession.

In this first case, a small group of faculty members in one department decided to be proactive and, in doing so, showed two unwritten tenets: (a) The academy is political, and (b) personal and professional networks are powerful informal forces.

Faculty members in many university departments around the country pay lip service to the concept of accepting students of color by claiming that they cannot find qualified applicants.

They insist that applicants of color are to have the same credentials as traditional applicants, many of whom come from more privileged backgrounds with fewer barriers to academic success. On this point, Bill commented, "But they never look for them. . . . Somehow they are to appear out of nowhere." Bill G. and colleagues knew that students of color with near perfect credentials were rare and that it was unrealistic to expect a large number of these applicants to choose this particular university department despite its national prominence.

Instead of passively waiting, Bill G. used the formal and informal culture of his university to find, recruit, admit, and train several cohorts of color. There was, of course, a formal admissions procedure and a formal set of university and department criteria in order to advance to and receive a degree. But there was nothing formal about using one's professional networks at other universities to find appropriate applicants of color, meeting and convincing the dean to provide recruitment and assistantship money, or using the provisional admissions tradition for applicants of color. There was nothing formal about making certain that these students were carefully counseled once admitted. Bill G. also knew that admitting these students was not enough: It was also necessary to guide them through the hidden rules of the department and university.

In our second case, the informal culture of the university was used to exclude a qualified scholar of color.

Case 2: When Excellence Is Not Good Enough

Professor Maria T., a Latina, was hired as a probationary faculty member. The criteria for retention and tenure at her university were (a) excellence in teaching, (b) scholarly productivity, (c) service to the university, and (d) service to the community. Over the next several years, she distinguished herself as a gifted teacher and adviser, and she served on many committees both in and outside of the university. When it came time for her tenure review, her colleagues were not enthusiastic about offering her tenure, even though the department committee recommended it. Her colleagues were concerned about the quality of several journals in which she had published and managed to have this concern reach members of the college review committee. The college-level committee voted against her tenure.

Maria T.'s experience is equally revealing about how the informal life of the university can be used to regulate participation. Maria T. did everything right with regard to the formal criteria for retention and tenure. But her case revealed a third unwritten tenet: Besides the political nature of her appointment and the use of networks to make decisions, hidden agendas reveal how formal criteria are likely to be used to get desired results.

Before Maria T. was hired, her colleagues wanted to hire another person whom they had groomed for the position. This person was going to be a core player in a research institute the department was planning. But the institute was shelved because of the department's declining undergraduate enrollment and cuts in university financial support to the department. Meanwhile, the department was under pressure from the administration to hire a minority faculty member. What Maria T. did not know, when she was hired, was that key faculty members viewed her as a temporary appointment and as a good way to improve the department's enrollment.

We might question the department's ethics. On the surface, it appears that nothing Maria T. could have done would have changed the outcome if she was not included into the long-term plans of her department. If the department committee did not have questions about her publications, they would have found something else. The department's hidden agenda needed to be made public, and Maria T. should have been hired to be part of the proposed institute. A temporary faculty person would have had little incentive to improve the department's enrollment and would not have addressed the administration's pressure for diversity.

The Power of Networks

In the first case, informal practices worked to produce a diverse graduate-student population. In the second case, the informal decision structure worked as well but with a different result. In neither case were the informal and behind-the-scenes actions apparent. If we have convinced you of the importance of the "silent university," we would like to now focus on how things get done informally in such a way that they either include or exclude people. Let's look at two more real-world cases that illustrate this point.

Case 3: Political Mentoring

Michael C., a European-American, held a prestigious chair in a prominent department. He was convinced that specific conservative national policies were needed to address poverty in the United States, but his past experiences in taking the lead on such advocacy were very trying. Michael C. had been branded a racist and on several occasions was the center of very embarrassing controversies. He and a colleague decided that the way to address this problem was to find persons of color to take the lead. After several years of looking, they found the right person. Michael C. and colleague sponsored this junior colleague up the ladder through two academic appointments, got appropriate reviews and publishers for his initial books, and saw that he was appointed to the right national committees and commissions. This man is now a prominent spokesperson for Michael

C.'s point of view. Michael C. is now able to continue exerting his influence, although he enjoys a less-public role.

████████████████████████████████████

In this third case, Michael C. illustrates how personal and professional networks are used to achieve an informally agreed-on agenda—and a conservative one at that. The person of color Michael C. sponsored had just the opposite experience as Maria T. in Case 2. This person was central to a group of prominent faculty members' agenda and therefore was supported. It was done informally, over a period of time, and completely through networks. In the same way, not becoming a part of the right informal networks can be detrimental, as in Jose J.'s experience.

████████████████████████████████████

Case 4: "I Told You So"

Jose J., a Puerto Rican, was admitted to a highly competitive Ph.D. program at a prestigious graduate university after the administration agreed to fund students of color. After Jose arrived, everyone was very cordial. He went to class, did assignments on time, maintained a B average, and worked with an assistant professor as his adviser. After attending the first two department socials, Jose stopped attending, feeling out of place at these boring events. The other (European-American) graduate students were always engaged in intense discussions about nothing of interest to Jose. Also, they gave the impression of working all the time. Jose did the same work, although more directly and with less effort. His intense discussions were with faculty and graduate students of color in other departments. After four quarters, Jose was told that it was doubtful that he would be admitted to candidacy and was advised to leave the program with a master's degree.

████████████████████████████████████

Like Maria T. in Case 2, Jose did what he was formally expected to do and still found himself on the outside. He neither tapped into his department's networks to learn its informal culture and expectations nor realized how political being a student was. But Jose's case revealed the fourth unwritten tenet: Perceptions matter. Jose appeared to not be working hard, to be uninterested in and unconnected to the issues, debates, and what was going on in the department. At minimum, he needed to have regular dialogue with faculty and other graduate students in his department. But also senior faculty should have reached out to help him integrate his interests into the department.

People of Color as Perceived Threats

We have encountered a fifth important dimension to the silent university's dealings with cultural differences: People of color are perceived as threats. This is true for more than often-cited reasons such as they bring down high academic standards. The more that admissions slots for students and tenure and tenure-track positions for faculty are viewed as limited and scarce, the less tolerance and more fear there is for "outsiders." Especially unsettling is "a minority presence" on campus that is not limited or controlled by European-Americans. One African-American woman's experience as a counselor illustrates this point.

Case 5: Do Not Be Too Successful

Toma J. was hired as a counselor in student services at a university with a past tradition of strong athletic teams. A high proportion of the males of color on campus were athletes. After a year, there was high praise for Toma J.'s work. But during the year, she discovered two things. First, African-American athletes had a high dropout rate, and those who completed four years rarely finished degrees. Second, there was a pool of local students of color who could gain regular academic admissions to Toma J.'s university, which was not as selective as many thought. Toma J. developed a proposal to recruit a small number of these academically qualified students of color each year. The proposal was warmly received by the dean and key faculty. But after it went to the president, the cheering stopped. It had been rejected. Toma J. was informed that she did not run the university and that the president and unnamed others would not "open" the university. Over the summer, Toma J.'s position was abolished in a quick reorganization.

By pointing out that there were African-Americans and other students of color who could gain admission through regular channels, Toma J. triggered the fifth tenet: People of color are a perceived threat to the status quo. Toma J. had exposed two things: (a) This "prestigious" university was, in fact, an elevated island of mediocrity, and (b) the president assumed that the university belonged to "traditional students and faculty" who were above the abilities and qualifications of people of color. For this university to act on its self-serving rhetoric was a threat to the claims of privileged, but simply average, European-American students who expected admissions to this prestigious institution.

Because fair-minded faculty and staff members did not have the necessary political clout, Toma J.'s only alternatives would have been to wait for new and enlightened leadership or use public exposure and outside pressure to embarrass the president into allowing the proposal to go forward.

A final case reveals yet another unwritten rule about how the university "manages" people of color.

Case 6: We Tried One Once and It Just Did Not Work Out

Mary S. and several of her colleagues (all European-Americans) in her department wanted to add a faculty member of color. They discussed this desire for a decade. Their concern was to find someone who had published quality work. It did not matter that they were a teaching faculty and that the candidates of color they interviewed had more publications than all but the most senior department members. Two years ago they finally hired a Chinese-American woman, but her employment was short-lived. They elected not to retain her, were displeased with her teaching, and felt that she was not happy with them. This young scholar pointed out that faculty sat in on her class but not in those of other faculty members. They had students give written reports only on her teaching. In addition, she was tired of their over concern about her family and personal life, their correction of her grammar in meetings, and that they did not provide constructive comments on early drafts of her papers.

When the department learned that the young scholar was leaving and without a fight, they were greatly relieved. The greatest part of their relief was that they would not be forced to hire a second person of color and then have two. That would have been too many. An additional tenet is now evident: Faculty members who have been with one another for decades constitute small insulated communities with long personal histories. Their relations with one another are professional only on the surface. Departments such as this are total institutions and insulate themselves from the "outsider" much as do police officers and firefighters, among others.

Departments have to make major psychological adjustments when new faculty arrive with familiar backgrounds and histories. So the informal workings and psychological isolation of department members are highlighted when they hire a person of color. Such an individual brings more than questions about what kind of work he or she will do or who he or she is. Besides taking a faculty line, this person also has an implicit invitation to become a part of the personal life of the department. He or she can meet the family, learn of personal likes and dislikes, find out about personal flaws and insecurities, and find out about department secrets and old scandals. Academic appointments are much more than professional jobs. They can be invitations into people's lives, living rooms, and private worlds.

What Can Be Done?

We will never do away with hidden agendas and networks, but we can do something about the extent to which they stay hidden and racially exclusive. We can also do something about the extent to which the real decisions about our careers are made in someone's living room or at the faculty club. We have found that hidden agendas vary in sophistication from very ambitious goals of influencing national policy or developing formal and highly regarded scientific theory to simply enjoying with colleagues and friends a relatively high income with minimal accountability and work.

One thing all hidden agendas and informal decision making cannot tolerate is public exposure, review, and critique. Exposure calls attention to the manipulation of university resources and the underlying motives for supporting, opposing, cooperating, or undermining formal decision-making processes. Getting hidden agendas out on the table identifies the current and desired future players, including whether any are people of color. It is also possible that a critique of the basic agenda might change the content of the agenda so that it will be to the department's advantage that others are included. Exposure also allows European-Americans as well as people of color to see and judge for themselves their institution's real position with regard to race. If nothing else, exposure, review, and critique of exclusionary and hidden agendas take away the justification for using the university as a formal front to advance a single racial or cultural agenda.

In principle, anything that exposes the informal culture of the institution and how it is used to maintain a monopoly of power and privilege is effective in showing the need for reform and for a level playing field for greater student and faculty diversity. We have seen students, faculty members, and administrators do many proactive things that work well to uncover the unwritten rules for others to learn, use appropriate networks, and address faculty fears. There are things that can be done to improve one's personal outcomes as well as institutional practices. What has fascinated us over the years is that anything that is done to improve outcomes and equity for people of color always also has the potential to improve outcomes for European-Americans. Everyone can positively benefit. Our advice is all proactive. Diversity in our departments will not happen without action on our parts. As Bill G. illustrated, it is really of no consequence to say and believe that we are fair-minded and not affected by institutional and cultural racism while keeping our departments or university racially and culturally closed and exclusionary by inaction.

Ideas for Improving Treatment of Students of Color

1. Find a successful model. There are demanding and prominent faculty members and departments that have been proactive and successful in recruiting and training people of color as students and hiring faculty. To say that you cannot find qualified students and faculty of color is a reflection of your own doubts, reservations, and lack of action.

2. Clarify your personal and department goals, plans, and agendas. Then make certain that diversity is part of them. It is all right to have an informal agenda, but it would be helpful if colleagues of color have a role in shaping these plans, goals, and agendas.

3. Use your professional and personal networks. One of the most common ways departments can put off their own responsibility for recruiting students of color is to hold the "administration" responsible for recruiting their students. Even if a good recruiter with a background in economics finds a prospective student in physics, that student is an outsider if the physics faculty does not know the student's professors and department.

4. To reach students of color requires funding. This is not because students of color need money to be motivated, but because most students of color and their families simply cannot afford to pay tuition *and* books, housing, food, clothes, and so on. Many cannot afford to have someone with a bachelor's degree and its earning potential not in the work force earning an income.

5. Bring good candidates to your campus to meet your faculty and graduate students. Students of color need to know what kind of environment the campus has. Is it hostile or livable? Are other students of color there for guidance and support? Will new students be accepted? You cannot learn these things from a handbook.

6. Do not leave advisement up to chance. Assign each student of color a proactive adviser who will periodically meet with him or her and give straight information and advice about how one succeeds in the department until a student has a chance to select his or her own academic adviser.

7. If a student has academic deficiencies, identify and correct them as soon as possible. It is reasonable to have some deficiencies in the first year, but if they carry over into subsequent years, the student's entire program can be called into question. What happens is that faculty and other students begin to talk about the student of color's weaknesses behind his or her back or do not want to be critical—until their comprehensive examination. Then it is too late. This only shows a breakdown in advisement or the fact that the department never really accepted this person as their student. (See Chart 1.2.)

Ideas for Improving Treatment of Faculty of Color

8. Make certain that people of color are recruited to be a part of your department's long-term goals and agendas and that they have

Chart 1.2 Improving Treatment of Students and Faculty of Color

Improving the Treatment of Students of Color	Improving the Treatment of Faculty of Color
1. Make recruitment and retention of students of color a priority.	1. Make recruiting faculty of color a priority.
2. Find and use a successful model to recruit and retain students of color.	2. Ensure diversity in all applicant pools.
3. Use your professional and personal networks to recruit students of color.	3. Use all networks to recruit and retain faculty of color.
4. Bring candidates of color to campus to preview environment.	4. Become a trusted and well-connected adviser.
5. Do not leave advisement to chance.	5. Make the criteria for retention and tenure clear.
6. Identify and correct academic deficiencies ASAP.	6. Make all decisions in the open.
7. Initiate and develop relationships with students of color.	7. Initiate and develop relationships with faculty of color.
8. Read ethnic journals.	8. Read ethnic journals.

a part in shaping those goals. If what you do is important, it will affect people of other races and cultures. Hiring faculty members of color for your department should not be the responsibility of the central administration, and it should not be one of those things your department does to appease the administration (for awhile).

9. Make decisions in the open where everyone in the department has an opportunity to participate. Racial and cultural differences within a department must be joined by a formal rather than informal process, because everyone is not part of the same social network.

10. Serve as a mentor, sponsor, or adviser. New faculty members of color need mentors who are well connected and knowledgeable about the informal culture of their department and university; this will help new faculty members to be retained or tenured.

11. Make the criteria for retention and tenure as clear as possible. If there is an area in academic life where there is a need for more objective measures and criteria, this is it. Even if it is unlikely that this problem will be addressed for the university overall, at least make your department's criteria clear and objective.

Chart 1.3 Strategies for Students and Faculty of Color

1. Know the political movers and shakers.
2. Network with professional, personal, and ethnic-specific groups.
3. Establish relationships within the department and the university.
4. Clarify your professional goals.
5. Watch for hidden agendas.
6. Seek out trusted senior advisers.
7. Identify discrepancies between your goals and the college's expectations.

12. Keep abreast of ethnic-focused journals and publications, particularly the ones in which your colleagues of color are publishing. We are surprised how often faculty members criticize these journals and yet have never actually read them. Like "mainstream" journals, they range in quality, difficulty in acceptance of articles, and points of view.

The information provided in Chart 1.3 provides useful tips for students and faculty of color in navigating the unwritten organization of the university. There are many more things that you can do, but the above are some of the things that can be done to use the informal practices of the university to promote diversity and to minimize the negative consequences of informal traditions and practices.

The next chapter addresses the question of racial identity and outlines the common myths about race. When we make reference to "whites" and "people of color," who and what are we talking about? This is not simply an exercise in definitions that you can skip over. It is central to what we need to know to make sense of the actions, inactions, and silent languages of everyone involved in all sides of the issues of diversity.

2 | What Did You Say You Were? Am I a Racist?

There is nothing more upsetting than being called a "racist." It is the modern equivalent of being tarred and feathered. It is a terrible no-win condemnation much like being asked "When was the last time you molested your child?" If you are accused publicly, your name and reputation can be seriously damaged. Some of your colleagues and even family will wonder about you. Many of us, in order to not risk going through this ordeal, end up avoiding certain teaching materials, shying away from open discussion of certain topics, and simply not saying what we think without going through the "Could *this* be interpreted as racist?" edit.

In the same way, there is nothing more degrading than feeling the bite of racial exclusion and putdowns made by even the most well-intended white colleagues. The victim of such behavior has three no-win choices. First, he or she can mention the offense in conversation, but this not only violates the middle-class European-American's social rule of politeness but also presents additional costs: Besides being considered rude and possibly maladjusted, the injured party usually will be ignored, excluded, or labeled a troublemaker from then on. Second, he or she can avoid speaking up. Say nothing long enough, however, and the victim is left to struggle with mounting internal anger, pain, doubt, and blame. Third, he or she can disassociate from other people of color and work toward being accepted as an individual apart from his or her race. This approach also has its price. The individual is never perceived simply as such. At best, this "honorary white" status lasts only as long as he or she is seen to be like a real white person and supports white interests.

Angry, long-suffering, and de-racial "blacks" are responding to how they are perceived by dominant European-American society. The most important point here is not that people of color respond the way they do. It is a response to whites. This issue is at the center of the dilemma of race in this country. Racism is maintained from generation to generation not simply because of economic gain and the preservation of white material privilege, but also by the necessity to maintain a belief in white racial superiority. The maintenance of physical racial purity grows out of a social identity built around our peculiar physical definition of race. The necessity to maintain racism also grows out of the way in which this identity must be insulated in order to remain unchanged. And we as educators either inadvertently reinforce and perpetuate racism or we challenge and work toward changing it.

This chapter is divided into three parts. First, we outline how racism has affected self-identity for European-Americans. Second, we show racism's related impact on the self-identities of people of color. And third, we describe the myths and realities of race. We have to talk about these issues. We have learned from listening, observing, and conversing with hundreds of students, faculty members, and administrators that both European-Americans and people of color have grown up with racial myths about themselves and one another. The myths were needed, held onto, and defended because we have inherited essentially racist racial identities. To effectively challenge the myths and their effect on education, we have to challenge our racial identities as well. Finally, by unmasking the myths, we open the door to the more authentic interracial dialogue on our campuses that is outlined in the following chapters.

Racism and Self-Identity for Whites

> What was fated to be the continuing crisis of my life, the crisis of racial awareness—the sense of being doomed by my history to be, if not always a racist, then a man always limited by the inheritance of racism, condemned to be always conscious of the necessity not to be a racist. To be always dealing deliberately with the reflexes of racism that are embedded in my mind as deeply as the language I speak. (p. 48)

Wendell Berry's quote offers one response to what it means to be white. We would add that it can mean being of European parentage; having a particular physical appearance; being native to particular European languages, customs, and foods; practicing particular European religions; and identifying with any number of European histories and communities. But there is a problem with these meanings. Given the tremendous diversity of customs, cultures, languages, and physical appearances among Europeans, of what utility is the term *white*? The answer to this question is buried in American history.

A "white" racial identity was necessary to maintain control in the early colonies. Initially, there was little distinction between the conditions of English indentured servants and African slaves who together were a clear majority of the population in key colonies. Together they had the potential to make demands regarding their labor or do much worse: to rebel. Social control in early America demanded three things. First, it was necessary to physically separate Africans from English and other indentured laborers. This could be accomplished by giving each group unequal statuses and intensifying slavery. Second, the different statuses for slaves and indentured laborers should be physically and immediately obvious: Skin color would do. Finally, Europeans should be united regardless of different status and cultural backgrounds. A so-called white people came into being—before the concept of an "American" became important after the Revolutionary War.

The term *white* was intended to disregard European cultural and historic differences. It was intended to stand for racial unity and superior social status based on physical appearance and ancestry. It was also intended to mean and convey overall racial superiority, physical separation, a community apart from others, and mutually exclusive long-term interests. The exclusion of Indians, Africans, women, and immigrant Europeans from early universities was an institutional expression of this cultural intent.

Some readers will dismiss this important history because of its implication or because it is history. But being white matters today as much as it did then. The same meanings are now part of our national culture and find expression in our university curriculum. It is no wonder that many Americans see themselves and others as physically distinct and unequal races or have to work so hard to deny it. Ismael Reed captures very well the racial myth of color, its utility, and its implications for all of us.

America's obsession with Black and White is nothing more than a myth created centuries ago, when African-Americans had to be seen as different from everyone else to justify their enslavement. But the intricacies of race, class, ethnic and nationalistic enmity go far beyond Black and White not only in America but worldwide. (Harrington, 1992, p. 418)

European-Americans are not the only ones affected by the myth of color. The myth cannot work for European-Americans, unless their redefinition of themselves as whites does not also define and blind people of color. One group cannot affirm or deny its assumed superiority if there is not also another group that has to affirm or deny its assumed inferiority.

Racism and Self-Identity for People of Color

"Niggers ain't shit."

Every Third World racial group that has been in the United States for more than two generations develops the equivalent to the above statement. It is a statement of self- and group hatred and limitation. It is the internalization of racism. You cannot be "black," "Latino," "Indian," or "Asian" and not struggle with internal racism. Your historic and racial identities are no longer mutually exclusive from the thinking and perceptions of European-American society. We can run from this fact, but we cannot escape. We can ignore it, but it is always there. To be a person of color in the United States is to be an outsider, a problem, unequal, and here to be used. To breathe this cultural air makes it necessary to struggle for spiritual, community, and physical survival. Also to be somebody and have positive regard for yourself and your race means going against the tide and necessitates resistance, defiance, and occasionally open rebellion.

For people of color to survive in America, it is necessary to do three things. First form a community by coming together to acknowledge and support one another. It is fascinating to see how people of color who acknowledge their history, community, and culture will greet one another despite being total strangers when they travel, are at school, at a conference or doing business. Second, form institutions that address your physical and cultural needs: churches, social clubs, beauty parlors, food stores, restaurants, and civil rights organizations. Finally, work very hard against internalizing anger and inferiority at how people of color are treated and regarded by white society. This is both a personal and collective effort.

Is there a way out and a way to break the need for such a struggle on the part of both European-Americans and people of color? We think there is. The key is in challenging the definition and meaning of race, and educators should lead the way. A prerequisite for changing racial cultures in this country is

Chart 2.1 Myths and Realities of Racism

Myths	Realities
1. There are three distinct physical races.	1. Racial differences are social, economic, cultural, and political.
2. Not everyone has a culture that matters.	2. Everyone has a complex culture that matters.
3. Racism is personal and happens in isolated instances.	3. Racism is personal, institutional, and cultural.
4. Affirmative action is reverse racism.	4. Affirmative action seeks to reduce racism.
5. Racism is an on-off phenomenon.	5. Racism operates on a continuum from overt to covert.
6. Racism must be conscious and intentional.	6. Racism ranges from conscious to unconscious.
7. A racist must be mean-spirited.	7. Racism ranges from mean-spirited to well-intentioned.
8. What happens to people of color is unimportant.	8. Our racial communities are interdependent.
9. Racism exists when European-Americans say so.	9. Racism can be identified by the victim, perpetrator, or observer.
10. "I couldn't possibly be racist because I have friends in other races."	10. You can be a racist and have friends in other races.
11. Racism is inevitable.	11. Racism is not inevitable.

to challenge the racist content of white social identity and the equal and related racist content of "black," "Indian," "Hispanic," and "Asian" social identities. In doing so, European-Americans and people of color need to address, initially through higher education, the national myths of race and the realities obscured by these myths.

The Myths and Realities of Racism[1]

Myth 1: There are three distinct physical races, each with innately conditioned and distinct aptitudes, talents, and behaviors that have social and economic outcomes. (See Chart 2.1.)

Many of us walk into our classrooms on the first day and look out over the visual landscape of students. We see our new students, but we also see their races. Based on prior experience, how they are dressed, where they sit and with whom, their body language and many other cues, we have hunches about them. The course begins and, except for a few surprises, they predictably distribute themselves on our grading scales more or less by race. How do you explain this? The people of color do not work as hard, have language problems, are poorly prepared. Or we do not see or try not to explain the disparity. Whether we have explanations or not, many of us dance around and are uncomfortable with the daily evidence of racial differences because we either believe deep down inside that innate physical differences do exist or we are struggling with not wanting to believe it.

Reality 1: The demonstration in society and the university of different outcomes with regard to aptitudes, talents, and behaviors by so-called races are due to social and cultural factors: (a) differences in historic social and economic status, (b) differences in present-day opportunities, and (c) learned assumptions about one's own color and racial potentials.

The differences between the races that we see in the classroom, in athletics, and in society are due to social circumstances and culture. Racial differences are not innate, because the races as we define them are not distinct physical populations or gene pools. The genes for particular skin color, hair texture, bone structure, and eye color are few and minor in comparison to all the other ways that we can differ within and between each so-called race. The reality of race is the following: We can assume that with a few exceptions, the vast majority of our students, regardless of race, have roughly the same innate potential. If we cannot make this assumption and wish to avoid it, then we have to entertain in fact or by default some form of innate racial differences. Alternatively, if we accept the assumption that there are no innate differences by race, then we have to reexamine two things: (a) our assumptions about the students in our classrooms and (b) our approach toward educating them.

If the differences between our students are circumstantial (largely economic) and cultural, our first challenge as educators is to understand those circumstances and cultural assumptions. Our second challenge is to devise ways to teach using what the students bring to the classroom. We already do this with middle-class European-American students. Most of us have not thought to do this with students from other backgrounds because we have assumed that they must first become like the "traditional student." This point leads to the second myth.

Myth 2: Not everyone has a culture, and if they do and it is not English, it is of little consequence, is simple and easily discernable, and will eventually disappear.

The first consequence of a belief in race as a physical phenomenon is that only the dominant culture is recognized. If other people have culture, it is simple and primitive in comparison to ours. With just a few terms and concepts, you know all you need to know in order to communicate. Certainly, by the third immigrant generation these cultures and language will disappear because they are of little consequence. The idea that any culture other than the English-American continues and has contemporary expression apart from dance, restaurants, and multicultural holidays draws for most a blank stare and is threatening. "We are one big culture, the American culture, and all this talk about 'Mexican this,' 'African that' is divisive."

Reality 2: Apart from the historic and contemporary consequences of racial discrimination, racial and ethnic differences are intersecting cultural threads.

Virtually all of us are to some degree English-Americans in our public and professional thinking and behavior. But only a few of us are only English-American in our private, community, and family lives. The reality is that race is cultural as much as European ethnicity is cultural. Apart from social class and circumstances, what distinguishes one "race" from the other are variations in historic attitudes, beliefs, values, and memories. The content and inner worldview of these cultures are learned. They are not acquired by nature, innate inheritance, or "blood" ancestry. This means that anyone from one race (culture) has the potential to learn elements of another culture despite being perceived as a member of another race. This person can even be accepted by members of the other race and participate in their social and cultural life just as an Italian-American has the potential to learn and then participate in Irish-American community life. The key is knowledge, being accepted, and then being allowed to participate. So a person of African descent has the potential to become a European-American in mind and participation just as a person of European descent has the potential to become an African-American.

There is one additional complexity. To some degree we are all already mixed in our racial cultures. While we may maintain racial group membership by physical appearances and acknowledged ancestry, we have already both consciously and unconsciously learned and internalized elements of one another's racial and ethnic cultures. So the students who enter our classrooms and laboratories may appear to be members of one or the other physical race, but they are in fact much more complex. They bring talents, sensitivities, and potentials that we cannot begin to tap until we accept, learn, and use their cultural diversity in our teaching. It is ethnocentric and racist to distance ourselves from them, take no responsibility for them, and give them anything less than our best because they do not come to us wrapped in middle-class and appropriately English-American trappings.

Myth 3: Racism is personal and now happens in isolated instances.

This myth sees acts of racism as occasional and flawed individual behavior, not as outcomes of cultural beliefs or institutional actions. Acts of racism occur in a vacuum and are performed by lone and misguided individuals. Organizations, institutions, and other racial groups do not perpetuate racism. Racial jokes on a campus radio station, racial slurs on the bathroom walls, racial epitaphs shouted from one student to another, or a department chair who jokes about seeing all African-American women as secretaries are simply isolated, random acts of lone individuals.

Reality 3: Racism is perpetuated and reinforced at three levels: the personal, the institutional, and the cultural.

If you believe in the third myth, no person or institution has to take any responsibility or acknowledge that racism is more than personal and does not just happen in isolated instances. Individuals in one race do not believe out of the blue or by happenstance that other individuals in another race are inferior to them or are automatically less qualified. No one is born with such an assumption. We get this belief from some place and it is learned not simply by isolated and random individuals, but by groups. Then group assumptions about race and self are either reinforced or dissuaded by institutional affiliations. There is no institutional neutrality or middle ground. The institution is implicated in racism to the extent that it ignores or encourages the racism of individuals and group members. To remain neutral is to condone racism. A do-nothing position perpetuates racism even though it does not directly encourage it. So however you look at it, you cannot separate the individual from group membership or from institutional influences.

Institutions perpetuate as well as redefine general cultural beliefs through their mission, how they are organized, and how they operate. For example, the University of Mississippi's racial segregation policies until spring 1963 were hardly independent of the white-supremacist beliefs of most European-American Mississippians. Individuals cannot be separated from institutions any more than a university can be separated from the general culture. We in the university either perpetuate racist beliefs within our culture by default or by affirming the status quo, or we work together to change the university and the culture as well.

Myth 4: Affirmative action and other preferential treatment programs are by definition racist in reverse.

We have collected comments from European-American faculty and staff members during recent visits to several campuses. They speak for themselves.

"I didn't discriminate against anyone else, so why single me out for punishment?"

"Those reaping the rewards of affirmative action haven't been slaves, so why reward them?"

"Affirmative action is reverse discrimination."

"It's just not right to consider one's skin color as more important than their qualifications."

"With all of this diversity, racism is now obsolete. We are all at the same starting gate."

"White men are losing their jobs because we are the wrong color."

"Maybe we should start a European-American support group."

Reality 4: European-American racial discrimination and overt racial restrictions against people of color unfairly limited access to social and economic opportunities in the past. The present inequities are the result of both past and continuing—and now covert—racial discrimination and restrictions.

We made striking progress in reducing racial inequality by eliminating legal separation of the races in employment, education, housing, and public accommodations in the 1960s. But the civil rights movement and the reforms that grew out of the movement did not eliminate racial inequality, especially in economic participation. In fact, since 1981, we have slid backward in several indices, including employment, health, and housing. To eliminate affirmative action and do nothing would do two things: (a) fail to address continuing covert racial discrimination and restrictions and (b) allow current inequalities to increase and continue into the foreseeable future. The differences we see in academic background and preparation among the races in our classrooms have more to do with differences in their family economic background and circumstances than racial culture or work ethics.

Myth 5: Racism is an on-off phenomenon: Either it is an overt, KKK type of act or it does not exist.

Somehow we believe that racist individuals are that way at all times and in all places. More important, if you are not a racist, there is no time or place that you can be. Racism is an all-or-nothing phenomenon. Racist behavior is very clear and obvious and on the order of cross burnings, Rodney King beatings, or obvious racial slurs. Alternatively, a hiring decision based on "merit" or a Eurocentric curriculum could not possibly be racist.

Reality 5: Racist acts fall along a continuum from overt to covert. They also range in intensity.

You do not have to guess about overt racism. Even though it is disturbing, it is authentic and clear. But as we pointed out in the first chapter, most acts of racism in the university are rarely direct, overt, and intense. They are indirect, informal, covert, and disgustingly civil. In most cases, people of color are left guessing. Even words are used with double meaning: "affirmative action hire, qualified minority, politically correct, financial aid student, and need to adhere to standards." Living with covert racism is like being penknifed a hundred times a day with indignities and reminders of your subordinate status. But the outcome of such indirect, covert, and civil acts of racism are just as effective in limiting opportunity and monopolizing power as in the "good old days" when we put the dagger through the shoulder blades.

Myth 6: Racism must be conscious and intentional to be called racism.

The logic of racial avoidance suggests that only when we are consciously thinking about the superiority and inferiority of people based on their race are we being racist. If history department faculty members never consciously intended to exclude all people of color from their course offerings but had accidentally done so, they would escape being called racist.

Reality 6: We can have explicitly racist intent and behaviors that range from being conscious to unconscious. Even the subconscious can have racist ideation.

We are amazed at how bright people who are ordinarily astute observers of the richness of human behavior become so dense when it comes to race. This is one of the few remaining areas in American life where people are still viewed as being innately good or bad. Racist behavior like any other behavior has a much more complex reality. We believe that the most virulent forms of racism are played out in our subconscious as we go about just being ourselves and "just doing our jobs." What ultimately gets expressed is only what comes to the surface. However, we can begin to check racism's influence on us just as we do other destructive beliefs and behaviors by recognizing and accepting that racism is embedded in our unconscious. Instead of denying and ignoring racism, we can become conscious and curious and ask how and in what ways racism reveals itself to others and to ourselves.

Myth 7: A racist must be mean-spirited.

This assumption most often surfaces in this form: "If I am well intentioned and care about people, then I can't possibly be racist." Respectable, well-intentioned, educated, and even liberal-minded people are opposed to racial exclusion.

Reality 7: Racism can range from very mean-spirited to the best of intentions.

We have found discussing this reality to be most helpful in understanding how racism works and is expressed. Once we acknowledge that there are very few mean-spirited persons in the academy, we can move on. We can affirm and accept each other's good intentions as real and then quickly move on to the impact that our behaviors have on others. Racism's bottom line is its negative impact on its victim(s) regardless of the actor's intentions. When individual good intentions remain the focus of the conversation, the impact of the perceived racism on the victim(s) cannot be discussed and is invalidated.

Myth 8: What happens to and goes on among people of color is of relative unimportance if it does not involve European-Americans.

This belief for avoiding racism and its implications holds that whatever happens between and among people of color is solely the result of their own will, choices, and actions. They are worlds unto themselves and totally responsible for both the good and the bad that happens to them. They are unaffected by what European-Americans think or do. The only exception to this belief is made when a European-American is involved. This exception is especially important if the European-American is "respectable" and middle class.

For example, in New York City, an African-American woman was raped by two attackers and thrown off a roof. Miraculously, she survived. There was little effort to find her attackers, and the incident was back-page news for one day. Shortly afterward, a European-American woman was raped in Central Park. Her alleged assailants were found, and this incident was front-page news for two weeks. Does being thrown off a roof make one rape less horrible, newsworthy, or worthy of police attention than being attacked in a park? Of course not. It was the racism of Myth 8: the attitudes of media, police, and the general public toward the races of the victims that made the difference in response.

Reality 8: Our racial communities are interdependent and largely overlap; what happens to and among people of color is important regardless of whether European-Americans are or are not directly involved.

A marvelous Douglas Turner Ward play, *Days of Absence*, ran in New York City in 1965. The play was a parody on what it would be like for the European-American residents of a small Southern town if all of the African-Americans disappeared. You can already guess that all of the essential dirty jobs were left undone. But what the play explored were the more important and less apparent nonmaterial dependencies. There was no one around to blame things on, to displace anger against, to tell secrets to, and to affirm one's higher standing. Also none of the European-American characters ever asked about or wondered what happened to the African-Americans. The European-Americans were only concerned with the implications of the African-Americans' absence for themselves. This nation may not be a small Southern town, but the material and psychological dependencies on the presence and subordination of people of color are still with us. Many European-Americans are still defining other racial communities only by their importance to them.

Educators who decry the poor preparation of students of color at the level below them are like the European-Americans in Douglas Turner Ward's small Southern town. Poorly prepared students of color define the bottom and show the failure of lower status and lesser trained teachers. Poorly prepared students of color also define how much smarter, better educated, and important European-Americans are. If poor preparation of students of color was the problem that we say it is and we cared, then we would organize and work to do something about it. But apparently the problem is not compelling because students of color are not racially or culturally "ours," and most of us believe that their failure and problems do not affect us or our racial and social class communities.

Myth 9: Intentions, actions, and outcomes can only be validated as racist by European-Americans.

To avoid racism and the contradictions in one's racial identity, you cannot allow others to define what is and is not racist. Therefore, people of color, especially African-Americans, are much too sensitive about alleged white racism. They are not reliable barometers for its existence. And so those who hold this belief state that people of color will use their race to disguise their own inadequacies, curry favor, or serve as a crutch. Some African-Americans have a similar view of European-Americans. Either way the conclusion is that the victim cannot be trusted to know what is or is not racist across race lines.

A recent example of this myth in operation is a newspaper report about an incident in Florida. An African-American man was kidnapped by three European-Americans, doused with gasoline, set on fire and burned over 40% of his body. A note was left that read "Compliments of the KKK." The news report went on to tell how authorities were investigating "whether or not the incident was racially motivated." Is nothing obvious! What does it take for something to clearly be "racially motivated"?

Reality 9: Intentions, actions, and outcomes can be validated as racist by anyone whether or not they directly experience it.

You do not have to be an African-American to realize that the kidnap and burning of the African-American man in Florida was racially motivated. To prevent such callous disregard, we suggest two strategies. First, adopt the approach taken very successfully in business: The customer is always right, and any complaints are worth prompt and thorough investigation. We contend that it should be the same with race. If someone European-American claims that they have been discriminated against or treated in a racist manner, do not automatically assume that they are wrong. Give the charge prompt and careful attention. Second, because they are conditioned to expect and disregard charges of racism against European-Americans from people of color, European-Americans should start calling one another on racism. Racist intent and actions are more apparent from within the group. In fact, racism cannot be acted out without implicit knowledge and the "neutrality" of others within the group. In the same way, people of color need to call one another on charges of European-American racism that come more out of anger than fact.

Myth 10: I could not possibly be a racist or do racist things because I have friends of other races.

Most of us will admit to having been brought up in households and communities in which people held overt or covert racist beliefs. But with few exceptions, European-Americans claim that if there was any racism expressed in their household, they did not learn it. In the same way, people of color claim that if there was any internal racism, they did not internalize it. We can all prove that we are incapable of racism by the friends we have and the people we know who are members of other races. We are all 100% pure and clean. Really? Are we not fooling each other?

Reality 10: You can be a racist and do racist things regardless of having friends in other races.

As long as our historic racial identities stay intact, we can do all sorts of things to affirm European-American superiority and continue the related inferiority of people of color. The irony is that it is not just European-American people who will consciously and unconsciously continue this history. Because none of us is racist or can do racist things, we can decry racism and act as if we are all the best of friends. We can mutually and collectively continue to fool ourselves by believing in the myths and ignoring the realities. But everything changes once we challenge our historic identity and begin to struggle against the extent to which we all have been racially conditioned. You realize that we have to be responsible for who we are and the impact of what we do regardless of intent. When this happens, we may lose some of our friends in our own and in other races.

Myth 11: Racism has always been with us, is inevitable, and will always be with us.

How convenient! Because people have always found some reason to hate, fight, and discriminate against one another, racism has always been with us. It is naive to think that we can now eliminate something that has always been with us. Racism is inevitable, and what is inevitable is likely to always be with us. This is yet another reason for not taking racism seriously and not taking responsibility of one's actions with regard to race.

Reality 11: Racism has not always been with us and, therefore, is not inevitable.

It just so happens that racism is relatively recent. Prior to Europe being cut off from the Mediterranean by Muslims, Africans were highly regarded in Europe as scholars, merchants, religious leaders, and diplomats. Even after the Moorish invasion of southern Europe, there was no evidence of a general belief among Europeans in "white" or "pan-European" superiority and all other peoples' inferiority. There was a prejudice of color as indicated in Shakespeare's *Othello*. If there had been racism as we know it, Othello would not have been respected as a nobleman and a general despite his complextion. The general belief that European-American peoples are superior to peoples of color was not articulated and codified in culture until there was a need to justify slavery and colonialism. So despite all our human flaws, it is quite possible to get along without racism. If we have any problems that are inevitable, racism need not be one of them.

> History, despite its wrenching pain,
> cannot be unlived, and if faced
> with courage, need not be lived again.
>
> —*Maya Angelou, U.S. presidential
> inaugural poem, January 1993*

What Can Be Done?

There is a need to bring to consciousness all of the daily and taken-for-granted assumptions about ourselves and others. We need to also become more skilled at uncovering the implicit meanings of the things said and done around us. This is hard work, extremely personal, and long-term. But there are things that we can all do to make it happen and make the experience interesting, personally liberating, and even fun.

Personal Things to Do

1. We strongly urge you to read about the early colonial efforts to control African slaves and European immigrants in the 1600s and early 1700s. Because the colonists never imagined that one day the population would be generally literate, they wrote very frankly to

one another about what they were doing and why. This is the period when our current racial identities were defined.

2. Ask yourself who you are culturally. This is not a question about your profession, individuality, philosophy, or ideals. This is a question about what historic and social group identities you affirm and are identified with by others.

3. Ask yourself who you would culturally like to be. Again this is not simply a question about individuality. Cultural questions are social ones. There has to be others who either are or will be like yourself. If you are not exactly who you would like to be, then what will you do to bridge the gap? Create a plan of action and do it.

4. Form a discussion and study group to discuss these issues and to read the growing literature in fiction and nonfiction that challenges and critiques racial and cultural identity in the United States.

5. When you hear racist or other harmful comments by persons in your own social and professional group, do one of two things. First, call attention to the comment with a question: "Do you mean that. . . . Have you thought about the implications of this point. . . . Have you done that?" Or second, challenge the speaker on the comment. In both cases, the speaker undoubtedly will say something to save face, but he or she might get the message.

6. Visit domestic cocultural communities by invitation and with sponsorship. Such a visit might be into someone's home, church, club, or neighborhood celebration. Be in the cultural and racial minority for a change. It is one thing to be an outsider observing. But it is another to have some degree of acceptance that allows you to question, converse, overhear, and see people acting out and enjoying themselves without editing their culture: that is, being who they are with one another.

Professional Things to Do

7. Personally investigate a "racial" incident on your campus. Talk with both sides if that is possible. See if any of the myths and realities discussed in this chapter are in operation. If you can see through to the conflict of intentions, fears, and actions, then you will learn a lot about your own attitudes and actions.

8. Have your department sponsor and organize a series of focus groups on teaching and learning. In each group the discussion leader

Chart 2.2 Becoming Literate in a Race-Conscious Society

Personal Doables
1. Read about the early colonial effort to control African slaves and European immigrants.
2. Ask yourself who you are culturally.
3. Ask yourself who you would like to be culturally.
4. Form a discussion and study group.
5. Actively address racist comments.
6. Visit and recognize the knowledge base of domestic cocultural communities.

Professional Doables
7. Personally investigate a "racial incident" on your campus.
8. Have your department sponsor and organize a series of focus groups on race and multicultural issues.
9. Pay special attention to students of color who appear to be at risk.
10. Look for your cultural biases in your teaching, grading, and advising.

and students should be of the same race to foster cultural identity. Ask them to talk about their perceptions of how they are regarded and treated as students by faculty members and other students. Then have them talk about the circumstances under which they enjoy learning. Compare how they are treated in class with what they expected and how they would like to be treated.

9. If any group of students consistently attends your classes or program unprepared, work with them. Do not ignore them or put them down (and doubly victimize them) because of institutional omissions. Then be one of those who actively gets the university or college to address the problem.

10. Look at the past three years of grades in your classes by race. Are they stratified and, if so, why? (See Chart 2.2.)

The idea of better communications leads us to the next chapter. It is an issue of particular importance to become more skillful in intercultural relations.

Note

1. For more discussion on this subject, see Auletta and Jones (in press).

3 | Communication, Communication, Communication!

Intellectually, we may know that the communication process is subtle, systematic, and multidimensional and that it takes place on two levels: the content (topic) and the relational (feeling and power). But, in fact, we forget this when we feel trapped in an interracial interaction, when we are being accused of being "culturally insensitive," or when we hear someone say, "This whole university is racist." It is at these moments that we feel vulnerable to others' interpretations. Then we become conscious of being in an "interracial relationship," of feeling defensive, uncertain, not wanting to offend, wanting to analyze the content, and needing to get away from the murky, uncomfortable arena of "race relations." It is no wonder that interracial interactions are described as walking on eggshells or across a minefield.

Communication: Racial Dividers and Connectors

Although we do not have the winning all-purpose multiracial strategy for effective communication, we will offer 10 interracial communication dividers and 10 corresponding interracial communication connectors (see Chart 3.1).

Chart 3.1 Understanding How We Communicate About Race

CONTENT MESSAGES
The topic; overt, verifiable message

RELATIONAL MESSAGES
Runs concurrently and communicates issues of power and feelings about self, others, topic, and situation

ONE-UP
Assumes control; superiority; right to judge, blame, and focus conversation

ONE-DOWN
Allows others to control, judge, blame, and label. Communicated by withdrawing or withholding ideas, attention, cooperation, support, and so on.

TWO-ACROSS
Allows all voices to be heard. Communicates high concern for self and others and takes a collaborative approach.

RACIAL DIVIDERS
One-up and one-down content and relational messages that communicate "Your experience with your race or gender does not matter, and learning about them is not my responsibility."

RACIAL CONNECTORS
Two-across content and relational messages that communicate "Our experiences with our race and gender and each other matter."

SOURCE: Adapted from systems theory, most notably Watzlawic, Beavin, and Jackson (1967).

In interracial interactions, power and race are woven together and significantly influence the tone and texture of the relationships. Within each and every interaction, in many subtle ways, we communicate which of us does and does not hold the keys to individual, relational, institutional, and societal power. We send verbal and nonverbal messages with regard to power, and we interpret others' messages as "one-up" or "one-down" in power or as "two-across," or equals in power.

We are often unaware when our messages are perceived by another as controlling, assuming that we are "in charge" and "right." These are one-up types of messages, or those that assume control, superiority, and the right to judge, blame, and monopolize.

One-down messages allow others to control, judge, blame, and label. When we accommodate or avoid topics and people because we fear the consequences or when we feel or act inferior or passive, we can be sending a message that we are one-down. People who feel one-down most often demonstrate their power by withdrawing and by withholding what scarce resources they do have, such as attention, cooperation, and support.

Racial dividers are the one-up and one-down content (topic) and relational (power and feeling) messages that can be perceived and interpreted as directly or indirectly saying, "Your experiences with your own race and gender do not matter. Learning about them is not my responsibility, it is yours."

Alternately, when we assume that all voices need to be heard, when we communicate a concern for ourselves and others and take a collaborative approach, we are sending two-across messages.

Racial connectors are the two-across content and relational messages that can be perceived and interpreted as directly or indirectly saying, "Your experiences with your own race and gender and your experiences with my race and gender matter. My experiences with my race and gender and my experiences with your race and gender matter. And learning about our individual and collective experiences is both our responsibilities."

Why Race and Power Matter

Every student and new faculty member experiences some anxiety, some feelings of inequity and of being in a one-down situation. The student and faculty member of color, however, often find themselves in an additional double bind that transcends the expected formal power alignment of senior to junior faculty, student to teacher. Yes, the professor has access to more knowledge than the student, and yes, the senior European-American faculty member knows more about the inner workings of the college than does the junior faculty member. But the feelings and interpretations of messages in interracial interactions include a heightened sense of the race and power dimension. It is a fact of history. It is also fact today: Students and faculty of color are more likely to accurately include race as a factor in interpreting power messages in communications.

1. "Why did the professor use that tone when he spoke to me? He did not use it with the white students."
2. "Why does the professor always look at me when he mentions the problems of the inner city?"
3. "Why am I asked to be the minority representative on so many committees? Am I the only one they can find?"
4. "I am told to devote my time to getting published, but then they keep asking me to speak in the community. Are white faculty members too afraid to go into the black community?"

Students and faculty members of color are more likely to consciously and unconsciously perceive, interpret, and articulate the racial and power dimensions of messages than are European-American faculty members and students. Our experience is that European-American faculty members are more likely to consciously ignore the racial and power relational dimension. Some feel guilty for being aware of it or assign it less importance, while still others acknowledge it but feel too self-conscious to honestly raise the issue as in "I just did not know what to say" or "I certainly do not want to offend."

Often by just not raising the issue of race, our messages can be perceived as belittling the importance of race and power. Even if we do not intend to send one-up messages, our words and actions are fair game for others to interpret and perceive them as such. We will outline 10 major types of messages that are likely to be perceived and interpreted by students and faculty of color as one-up or one-down racial dividers that can distance, discourage, and destroy interracial relationships. We also present the 10 corresponding two-across strategies that are more likely to contribute to an environment that connects, approaches, and encourages the honest discussion of racial issues. We do this by "unpacking" five interactions. Although you may not have experienced all of these actual situations, our research and our experiences on campuses across the country suggest that these stories are accurate and representative. We encourage you to think of the variations you have experienced.

Interaction 1: The Writing Lesson

Professor Lincoln is a European-American male senior professor who prides himself on being a good teacher of writing and for recruiting and mentoring students of color in the field. One day after class, Joyce, an African-American female aspiring to get into the graduate program, approaches Professor Lincoln and says, "Can you please tell me why I got a B on this paper?" Lincoln, who is in a hurry but wants to help anyway, asks another student, a European-American male who got an A on the assignment, to loan his paper to Joyce. Lincoln says to Joyce, "Here, read this paper. You two say the same things, he just says it in an A way." Joyce tells one of her other professors later, "Where does he get off, telling me that my writing is not as good as the white student's when we say the same thing. If all this department wants is to teach everyone how to become good little white people, then forget it."

Has the professor made some terrible faux pas? Is the student overly sensitive? Whatever the case, a well-meaning European-American male professor does not know that he offended a student of color and that his remarks could contribute to her leaving the program. The student of color feels isolated, alienated, and put down because of her race and wonders about her abilities to make it in the university. Let us look at this interaction more carefully, using our awareness of power messages embedded in communications.

Divider 1: It is not the color of a person's skin that matters, it is the content of his or her character.

Martin Luther King, Jr.'s noble and visionary attitude is often misinterpreted to mean "I don't need to think about what your being African-American, Chinese-American, and so on means to you or me. I can look past your cultural and racial identity." Professor Lincoln assumed, as do many of us, that the biological and psychological universals that do bind us are the most important. Such an assumption negates an important part of a person's experience with the world. In Chapter 2 we saw how, as European-Americans, we tend to take our ethnicity for granted, treating it as the norm because our culture dominates education, business, media, and the economy. Professor Lincoln is completely unaware that Joyce, as an African-American, would notice or care whether the A paper comes from a European-American or an African-American. He was oblivious to her possible one-down interpretation that "being black is not good enough."

Divider 2: Knowledge is neutral and objective, and I am not culturally or personally biased.

This divider may strike a nerve for many of us because it is controversial in several disciplines. However, let us look at this divider from the relational perspective of the student. When a professor uses only his or her own cultural background to communicate experiences as the basis of knowledge and excludes the experiences of others, that professor has dismissed all of the histories, experiences, and bases of knowledge outside of his or her own narrow racial and social class culture. When this happens, the student feels left out and put down: "My experiences or groping with how this knowledge relates to me and my people does not matter."

Professor Lincoln prides himself on teaching students to become "good writers." He is considered by many to be an elegant writer, so he operates on the assumption that the way in which he grades writing is the objective, right, and appropriate way to express oneself. If questioned, he will acknowledge that there are many excellent writing styles. But, in fact, he practices and teaches only one way to write. If he felt that his practice limited his skill and insight as a teacher and person, then he might become a better teacher who could better communicate with and help the Joyces in his classes.

Connector 1: Experience with one's own race, gender, culture, and social class matters.

I may not know how or in what ways that race, gender, and class matter to an individual. How can I find out? How can I be more sensitive to students of color?

It is ironic that our advice applies to all students. Using the connector above as a guide, Lincoln might hypothesize as follows: "Joyce is one of the few African-Americans in my class and one of even fewer majors. She may be more aware and sensitive to racial difference than I am. I know I can help her with her writing. Let me think about how to do this." He is much less likely simply to hand Joyce a white student's paper and say, "You two say it the same way. He says it in an A way."

Connector 2: Knowledge is contextually based, and my students' experiences with the knowledge I present may be different from mine.

How can I learn more about how students relate to and feel about this material? How can I use the fact that knowledge is culturally and personally influenced to reach out to students?

Armed with these types of questions, Professor Lincoln is likely to read Joyce's paper more carefully the first time, or, if not, to ask to reread it when Joyce approaches him. He will question and assess his own criteria in line with Joyce's writing strengths and weaknesses. Perhaps he will outline and discuss basic writing principles and then assist Joyce in exploring ways in which her voice and style can benefit from applying the writing principles. Perhaps Lincoln could do one lecture and assignment on the relationship of language to a person's life experience.

Interaction 2: It Is Your Responsibility, Not Mine

Faculty members are gathered for a meeting. In attendance are three European-American females, four European-American males, and one African-American male, a recently hired tenure-track assistant professor. During the report session, Jane commends an African-American female lecturer, who is not at the meeting, on her fine performance as mistress of ceremonies for the African-American graduation. Jane also mentions that she is disappointed that the department had so few African-Americans graduating. At this point, department chair Dr. Mark, pointing to the newly hired African-American male, says, "Well, that is why we hired Ross. We expect him to bring in 15." Dr. Mark laughs, but no one joins in. Then Dr. Tommyette, a European-American female known to be "anti-affirmative action," says, "Why would the blacks have a separate graduation? Maybe we should have a white graduation, too." What should Jane's response be? Ross's? Others'? What might the repercussions of this and similar types of messages be?

Divider 3: My job is to teach my courses (do admissions, etc.). I am not responsible for equity and multicultural issues.

Dr. Mark's comment clearly reflects his version of Divider 3: "My job is to chair the department, not recruit students of color." Although communicated in a joking manner, Dr. Mark's relational message can be easily interpreted as one-up. In other words, "I will control the conversation by making light of the topic at the expense of another."

This divider assumes that multicultural and equity issues are a separate and isolated job, activity, or goal. Multicultural and equity issues are seen as tangential to a university education. It is an add on, a tack on. This divider gets communicated throughout the university. Professor P. tells students that "Intercultural issues in philosophy is a fad." Or Professor D. assures us, "I teach constitutional law, so multicultural issues are not relevant." Or the chair of the academic senate says, "If we establish one 4-unit course in cultural groups and women and we have an ethnic studies department, then we have taken care of the multicultural issues." These one-up messages assert control over what is or is not the one "rightful" place for multicultural issues, and they unquestionably assume that its one place should not be in the center of educational consciousness.

Divider 4: You are solely responsible for your race and gender.

All too often, equity, race relations, and affirmative action are perceived as the sole domain of people of color. Colleagues of color from across the country tell us of their discomfort and anger at always being looked at for "the opinion" on race relations or on Asian-Americans or for being held responsible for the students of color in the department or the other faculty members of color in the university. This anger is especially fueled when all of these activities are either ignored or devalued in the promotion and tenure process. Being in a spotlight position is intensified for faculty members of color when they are the only ones to speak up for race and equity issues in a meeting. Their comments are either challenged or ignored but are rarely discussed in the same two-across manner as the need to obtain computers for all faculty members. This divider is a double bind. People of color can and do serve as important role models and sources of information for their own personal experiences with race, and yet they are the victims of the inequities of the system and should not be the primary parties responsible for fixing the problem.

We see Dr. Mark falling prey to this divider by joking that Ross was hired to "bring in 15" of his kind. The other faculty members can assume that they do not have any responsibility to recruit African-Americans. And Ross can internalize, "Maybe I am expected to increase the numbers of African-Americans in the department. I wonder if that was why I was hired? How seriously should I take this? If I raise the issue with the chair, he may deny it, and can I trust him?" Let us look at how the connectors could change the dynamics.

Connector 3: Equity and multicultural issues permeate everything in higher education.

Find out more about how to authentically integrate equity and multicultural issues into the university. Using this principle, Dr. Mark might not have made light of the observation that there are too few African-American majors. Rather he could have suggested and followed through on the idea that achieving ethnic diversity in the major is an important subject and needs to be placed on the agenda for discussion. Such a simple acknowledgment, for the moment anyway, would

have sent a two-across message that confirmed the importance of the issue and that it required everyone's involvement, even the involvement of those who disagree.

**Connector 4: We are all multiculturally illiterate, and we are
each responsible for knowing and speaking for ourselves and
learning about others.**

How can I understand another's experiences with race and
gender without making him or her the spokesperson for his
or her race? How can I come to understand and communicate that race relations is an important European-American
challenge?

Clearly, Dr. Mark should not spotlight Ross as the responsible party for African-American recruitment. Ross might well
be on a committee or serve as a consultant to the committee,
but that committee needs to be multicultural in its makeup
with European-Americans who both have power in the university and truly value equity as a priority. If Dr. Mark had
put himself in Ross's seat as an African-American faculty member at the meeting, he might better predict Ross's possible
responses.

Moreover, it is not just Dr. Mark's responsibility to communicate in an inclusive manner. To allow racial dividers to go
unchecked is to support them. Faculty members in similar
situations can counter with a two-across message to the chair.
In a private or public exchange, the message could be "I think
that all of us are responsible for creating a diverse student
body, not just Ross. Let us form a committee or discuss it in
a meeting." Or "I did not find that remark particularly helpful or humorous. Issues of affirmative action are serious, and
I hope we schedule time for a serious discussion."

We believe strongly that European-American faculty must
be willing to check their own and others' racial dividers.
Failure to do so further perpetuates Divider 4, that people of
color are the only ones responsible for raising the equity
issues. Issues of diversity are not just issues for people of

color. European-Americans have to take responsibility for these issues as well.

Interaction 3: The Educated Person

In an academic senate meeting, a new option in multicultural education comes up for a vote. The option includes the following required courses: "Prejudice and Discrimination," "Racism in Education," "The Multilingual Classroom," and "Educating the Community." A heated debate ensues. Professors Quinn and Tommyette argue, "We should be training our teachers in more of the classical Western civilization tradition because it emphasizes the democratic principles that unify us." Tommyette extends the argument to say, "To teach all these ethnic classes means we teach fewer of the classics. We are losing sight of our standards. Dinesh D'Souza and others clearly show that multicultural education and a focus on racism and oppression lowers the standards. We want to be proud of our quality education." Professor Smith, an African-American female faculty member, argues, "Standards, quality education, and excellence may be universal values, but the criteria for establishing these values are personally, culturally, and institutionally bound." Professor Johnson, an African-American male faculty member, states flat out, "Racism and oppression are worthy of study and to think otherwise is clearly racist." Professor Gomez, a Latina and associate dean, frames the multicultural education option in terms of statewide and national trends. The option passes with a slim majority vote.

Divider 5: Standards, quality education, and excellence are universal values and can only be upheld by maintaining the current core curriculum.

We all want to adhere to high standards of excellence and quality in education. This is universal. However, we often suffer from what Bourdieu and Passeron (1990) call "genesis amnesia," in that we forget how the standards became the standards. The standard college curriculum has changed over time. We used to teach only the Greek and Roman classics, and change from that was a concession because so many middle-class students were coming to college without tutoring in those essential works before leaving home. Today's introductory courses in the disciplines were considered "remedial" when they were introduced after the turn of the century. Then offering elective courses was the final blow to mandatory classicism. As times changed, so did the curriculum. Those who stood in the way then also used "maintaining standards" as their excuse.

Professors Quinn and Tommyette believe strongly in their one-up messages: "My interpretation for standards and excellence are right and do not include multicultural or racial issues, so therefore I have the right to judge what you do as substandard." Professor Tommyette teaches from this unquestionable one-up attitude that "Quality education is Western European and Western European-American traditions only." She critiques the contributions of other cultural groups from the European-American canon she calls "universal." She is known to make snide remarks that the "lack of ethnic scholarship is due to the lack of quality subjects to study." Students of color tell us that they feel one-down, distant, and awkward around her and try to avoid taking her classes. For many students and faculty of color, professors such as Tommyette and Quinn represent the worst in Eurocentric arrogance and send the strongest of one-down messages to people of color. Colleagues of color and European-Americans doing research and teaching in the multicultural arena hope she will not be in a position to judge or evaluate their work because she believes that studying about race and gender is divisive and political and therefore unworthy of academic pursuits.

Divider 6: Racism and oppression are political issues. Education is not political.

This divider clearly serves to squelch the academic and scholarly discussion of racism, sexism, and oppression. To include these issues as one of the lenses for understanding our world means that we see how European-American policies, programs, and practices influence groups of people based on their race and gender. This divider communicates that adding race and oppression to the critical framework does not contribute to our intellectual breadth or depth.

This divider also reflects the anti-intellectual bias that pervades discussions of racism among faculty members. Many of our most well-intentioned and caring faculty members admit to enjoying discussions of race, oppression, and multicultural education, but they neither want nor feel any urgent need to read about it. This one-up attitude allows faculty members to define racism and oppression as political or as personal feelings, thereby ignoring the vast literature on these subjects.

Clearly, Tommyette and Quinn communicated to their senate colleagues who teach these courses or who integrate these subjects into existing courses that they were "not teaching college-level material." Such a one-up message engenders a one-up response from Professor Johnson, who then labels Quinn and Tommyette as "racist."

Professors Quinn and Tommyette are unlikely to change their opinions. However, they and their colleagues need to know that their messages are contributing to the racial divide. Let us look at the connectors that do exist in this situation.

Connector 5: Standards, quality, and excellence are individual, institutional, and cultural agreements and challenges.

These are not godlike hand-me-downs, but individually, institutionally, and culturally determined. How can I explore and question the origins of the current criteria? What do these criteria really mean to me and to a changing university?

Professor Quinn and Tommyette could share their reservations in genuine two-across questions, such as: "I've never had any experience with these types of courses. Could you tell me about the curriculum, the assignments, and some of the ways in which you handle class discussions and evaluations?" Then the floor is open for exploration rather than explosion. Given that Quinn and Tommyette could not do so, Professor Smith clearly articulates the necessary connector and is further supported by Professor Gomez's example of how the "standard" for an "excellent" education for teachers is changing across the state and the nation.

Connector 6: Racism, sexism, and oppression are human experiences throughout history and across every culture.

How institutional and cultural power is used to oppress based on race and gender is not only worthy of study, but also sorely needed. How can I learn more about racism and sexism? When will I find the time? This is not my area of expertise. How can I get over my fear of being called a racist just for asking a question or making an unintentional offense?

Clearly, this connector is one of the most difficult ones to pursue given the anti-intellectual bias and the high emotional content of the issue. However, if we are willing to read and learn about the history of racism and the current oppressive practices, we begin to get far more comfortable addressing these hot topics. Just admitting that one is afraid of or knows very little about the topic goes a long way. Moreover, such a connector would allow us to question and explore with Professor Johnson the reasons behind his labeling Eurocentric curriculum as racist.

Interaction 4: Students Are Not What They Used to Be

Professor Green, a senior European-American faculty member, tells his class that the "essay exam will be based on your ability to synthesize the material in response to the question." Tammy, a 26-year-old Latina from a lower-middle-class upbringing, asks, "What do you mean 'synthesize' the material?" Green replies, "Analyze it."

At exam time, Tammy and several other students summarize the material and give examples of how they personally relate to it. Tammy gets her exam back with a C grade and is horrified. She studied so hard. She confronts Green, who says, "This is a summary, not a synthesis or analysis." Tammy says, "I don't understand the difference." Green, in a frustrated tone, tells her then (and the rest of the class the next day), "It is not my responsibility to teach you how to analyze, compare, contrast, and synthesize. If you are unprepared, that is your problem, I do not have time to teach you how to write and think." Class morale plummets. Tammy leads a group of students to the chair's office to complain. European-American students see Green as a "jerk." Students of color see him as a "racist jerk."

Now Professor Green may seem more abrupt than most on this issue, but he voices the frustration and belief that many of us feel and communicate every day to our students.

Divider 7: If you want to succeed here, you must adapt and change. After all, when in Rome do as the Romans do.

Expecting students to change is part of the learning process. We walk into our classes with a prepared syllabus: The guidelines, assignments, and assessments are set before we even know our students. We have a certain amount of material that must be covered during a term. We must get through it.

All of this may be true, but we get lulled into the position that the students must do all the changing and that adhering to the standard means not changing. This one-up message from the professor declares "I do not need to adjust and change to you." The student feels one-down: "My educational needs are less important than the professor's agenda."

Professor Green believes and communicates that his students must do all of the changing. Moreover, his frustrated and short tone of voice fuels the students' one-down, put-down feelings. Students of color, who have had such run-ins before, connect their feelings with racism and assume the worst.

Divider 8: If you do not meet my prerequisites, then it is not my responsibility to mentor you.

This divider is the correlate to Divider 7. Many of us are irritated and challenged by the varied levels of preparation of our students. When coupled with large classes, it becomes difficult to treat all of our students as individuals. However, when we do not, we place the entire burden of their education on them. And for students of color, the isolation is intensified by the additional racial and power dimension. Students hear variations of Divider 8 as one-down messages: "If you do not get it, then it is your fault. If you do not have the skills, it is not my responsibility (or desire) to teach them to you. Go away, go elsewhere. I do not want to teach you that skill. Your individual challenges are unimportant to me."

Connectors 7 and 8: Change and adaptation is a two-way process in a multicultural society and requires collaboration, a sharing of power, and a sharing of responsibility.

These connectors need to be communicated in our talk as well as our walk. We need to be willing to experiment and adapt to our changing student body. Together, as faculty and students, we must explore new ways of teaching and learning that reflect a shared responsibility.

Green could have acknowledged his challenges and communicated using Connector 7. For example, he could have said, "By 'synthesis' I mean. . . . Let us take a sample question and walk through the differences between summarizing, categorizing, comparing, and synthesizing." By doing this, Green not only has given the students the method that underlines his criteria for how to answer a question but also has adapted to the students. For those who do not know this skill, he has introduced it to them; for those who already know it, he has reminded them and shown them his preferred method of synthesis. He could bolster the connections by communicating a version of "I know some of you have had more experience with writing essay synthesis types of exams than others have. I will review the steps in class, and then for those of you who need more practice, write me a sample synthesis response and bring it to office hours and I will go over it with you and give you suggestions." Here Green has acknowledged the students' varied preparation and spent some but not a lot of class time introducing or reviewing the skill he expects. He acknowledges without judgment the need for individual attention. Green provides more office hour time; the student has to go the extra mile to prepare a sample for Green to critique. The effect of these types of two-across messages is clear. Hope for success increases, and Green, the students, and the chair are saved the embarrassment, disappointment, and anger associated with a lost opportunity.

Interaction 5: The Layoff Committee

Because of a depressed economy, for the first time in 20 years a midsize university has had to convene a layoff committee. With the exception of one African-American male senior faculty member, Professor Lawrence, the committee is entirely European-American and equally divided between males and females. Lawrence regularly questions the committee's assumption that the seniority principle should prevail. He argues that seniority will lead to de facto discrimination because faculty of color and European-American females have been the most recently hired. Each time he raises the issue, the committee members nod and mumble, "Of course, we will consider affirmative action," and then move on in the discussion, ignoring Lawrence's comments.

Finally, several students, faculty and staff members of color, and a couple of European-American females organize and, although not committee members, begin to attend the meetings and voice their support for Lawrence's concerns.

While many arguments were presented, let us summarize those that illustrate the two remaining dividers and connectors. Many of the committee members argued, "Seniority is the fairest principle because it treats everyone the same. To lay off using race and gender as criteria is to discriminate and be a reverse racist."

Divider 9: Equality means treating everyone the same.

By arguing that everyone should be "treated alike," many of the committee members were denying that layoffs by seniority would disproportionately affect faculty of color and European-American females. Others recognized the disproportionate nature but argued that it was a necessary evil. What many found so disheartening was the lack of genuine acknowledgment that layoffs by seniority would create problems of racial and gender equity and that perhaps together they needed to work on a different solution.

Connector 9: Equality and fairness means redefining criteria of excellence so that they can be equitably applied to everyone without exception.

Because race and gender continue to be barriers to attainment, equity requires that action must be taken to eliminate these barriers. The coalition of faculty and staff members of color created more inclusive criteria for faculty layoffs. Excellence in teaching, research, and publications were commonly shared and given higher value than seniority. However, *excellence* included excellence in teaching to a diverse student body, and excellence in research included contributing to the university's multicultural literacy. With such criteria, the nonproductive and mediocre teachers, regardless of rank, should be targeted for layoffs. Faculty members of color and women could live with this criteria. They were more often junior faculty and had to be productive and good in class to be retained. Alternately, it was noted that many highly paid senior faculty members were poor instructors and had not produced in years. It was unfair to the productive and good instructors in all ranks and backgrounds for mediocre faculty members to be retained. These superior and more inclusive criteria would not allow layoffs by seniority to preserve the "old boy" system in which clearly mediocre senior faculty could hide behind more productive colleagues.

Divider 10: Focusing on race and gender is divisive.

This divider judges the mere topics of race and gender as necessarily bad and to be avoided. The debate pits particularism (multicultural issues) against unity (common Western European-American traditions). The fallacy of this divider lies in its forced choice: We can only ignore race and gender or destroy the union. Somehow to acknowledge race and gender as a significant issue is seen as more divisive than ignoring it.

Connector 10: As cultural and equity issues, race and gender are important factors and should be considered along with other criteria in all institutional decisions.

The layoff committee was surprised and embarrassed when a "rainbow coalition" presented such simple, compelling, and inclusive criteria for layoffs. The point is that excellence and productivity were important criteria along with racial and gender equity. The criteria for such an important and unpleasant decision (laying off faculty members because of fiscal cutbacks) were not allowed to include seniority as a false proxy for excellence versus affirmative action. Race and gender equity and a more specific criteria of excellence were found and considered together. The layoff committee reluctantly adopted the criteria of excellence across the ranks. But it was clearly not what committee members wanted to do. The prospects of targeting long-time friends and colleagues for layoffs was just too unpleasant.

Many of the committee members left feeling that they were the victims of the "politically correct" (PC) movement. And going into the process, many of the European-American committee members were generally perceived by faculty members and students of color as well-meaning team players. However, because so many racial dividers were initially injected into the discussion, many of these same faculty members are now perceived as less well-intentioned and with more suspicion. They were perceived as combative, and their messages were perceived as one-up racial dividers: "Whatever race and gender barriers you have overcome and regardless of how good you are as a faculty member and scholar, it does not matter." Now the "rainbow coalition" of students and faculty are perceived as "potentially dangerous."

Yes, the wounds are still radiating. And yes, this was a particularly uncomfortable conflict. But because connectors were communicated and accepted, there is hope. We will revisit this important discussion again and again on campuses across the country. Conflict is the way we change.

In closing we are reminded of the Hasidic story that finding God is as easy and as difficult as finding our way home. Part of finding our way home is the getting lost, because when we are lost, we wake up and pay attention to our surroundings. The road to effective interracial relationships is as easy and as difficult as finding our way home. We must know when we are lost, wake up, and pay attention to the racial conflicts that are all around us. (See Chart 3.2.)

In Chapter 4 we will address some of these major conflicts.

Chart 3.2 Racial Dividers and Connectors

Racial Dividers	Racial Connectors
1. It is not the color of a person's skin that matters.	1. Experience with race, gender, culture, and class matters.
2. Knowledge is neutral and objective.	2. Knowledge is contextually based.
3. I am not responsible for equity and multicultural issues.	3. Equity and multicultural issues permeate everything in higher education.
4. You are responsible for your race and gender.	4. We are all multiculturally illiterate.
5. Standards, quality, and excellence are universal values.	5. Standards, quality, and excellence are individual, institutional, and cultural agreements.
6. Racism is political and education is not.	6. Racism deserves to be studied.
7. When in Rome, do as the Romans do.	7. Change and adaptation is a two-way process.
8. It is not my responsibility to tutor you in prerequisite skills.	8. Education requires shared responsibilities.
9. Equality means treating everyone the same.	9. Equality means redefining the criteria of excellence.
10. Focusing on race and gender is divisive.	10. Race and gender issues are integral to knowledge and all institutional decisions.

4 | Dealing With Conflict and Diversity in the Academic Community

Volatile conflicts around race, ethnicity, and gender issues and their attendant values are inevitable. So is the fact that we will be changed by these conflicts whether we like it or not. What is not inevitable is whether the changes that will result from these conflicts will be productive or destructive. How can we harness the energy of these conflicts? How can we resist the temptation to be "civil" and "genteel" just to avoid confrontations? How do we resist the temptation to use our position, power, and prestige to define these conflicts in ways that ensure our one-up position and perhaps unknowingly place both students and faculty members of color in one-down positions? How do we avoid blaming others for the problems we may be causing? Unlike the civil rights and antiwar movements of the 1960s, whose issues were clearly identified, the conflicts we face now on our campuses are amorphous and tangled. We often feel overwhelmed and are tempted to dodge, shift blame, or ignore the conflicts that arise.

It is not easy being a university professor during these times of budget cuts, larger classes, and increased diversity. It is not easy teaching students who are so diverse and who come to the university from different worlds than most of us.

We mastered our disciplines in Eurocentric institutions far from where our students come. We were mentored and tutored by mostly European-American professors. And, for the most part, we know so little about our students, their cultures, and their experiences. Such conditions do not make us bad people.

In this chapter we assume that increased racial and cultural conflicts are inevitable in the academic community. Therefore we must learn how to identify and use these conflicts as an opportunity for creative personal and institutional change.

Chapter 3 dealt with the day-to-day messages that serve to divide or connect people in interracial interactions. This chapter will focus on four major controversial and recurring "diversity" conflicts. Sometimes we will use a particular case study, other times a series of examples. While the ways in which these conflicts are played out on your campus may vary from our cases, we invite you to attend to the basic content and relational structure of the issues and apply the strategies to your particular situation.

The Purpose of Education

Content Issue

Students of all racial and social class backgrounds come to the university in search of knowledge and skills that will be useful in lifting them out of poverty and into the mainstream. They frequently see the purpose of higher education as providing them with the practical knowledge and tools to transform themselves and their communities. Most of all, they expect to get a good job. Many faculty members, on the other hand, see students of color as being ill prepared and as taking up space that should go to more deserving students: "You know the ones. The students who delight in the joy of learning. Those who love our disciplines as much as we do."

Relational Issues

When the conflict between education's practical and esoteric natures occurs between a student of color and a European-American faculty member, the dynamics are magnified. As faculty members, we may be quicker to see students of color who question the practical uses of knowledge or who appear withdrawn as evidence of their lack of understanding and preparation for being in the university. When we do this, we fuel the fire with our own one-up attitude of blaming the students. On the other hand, students of color are likely to be confused by professors who ignore or put down their wanting to know about the practical application of the knowledge they are learning. They may, in turn, see us as hostile, as attempting to keep them away from their goal of education. When such a conflict does occur, it usually does so in a context in which the faculty is European-American, the curriculum is Eurocentric, and administrators and other people in power positions are also European-Americans. Students of color can easily be reminded of their historical and current subordination in our society, and they may one-up the professor by concluding the worst: The professor or the university (or both) is racist.

We certainly mean no harm by our view of education as enlightenment, and we will be upset if told our attitude or behavior is being perceived as racist. The student nonetheless feels offended and put down, and he or she may internalize and interpret the situation as racist. Perception is quite important.

Recognizing the Conflict From the Student's Perspective

In interracial situations the professor cannot count on students who may experience the conflict to come forward and clearly lay out the grievances. However, the conflict and the students' perception of it do get expressed. Middle-class faculty members need to know that questions regarding applicability such as "How will this help me on the job?" or "How does this information relate to my experience?" are warnings to slow down and attend to the possibility of a perceived conflict over the purpose of education. Students who are combative, have "an attitude," score poorly on exams, come to class late, and even fall asleep are also signals that conflict is brewing. The conflict content may or may not concern the purpose of education. However, these types of relational messages signal loud and clear that the student feels one-down, left out, and uncomfortable.

How to Recognize the Conflict From the Faculty Perspective

When we observe such behavior, we should resist our tendency to label, judge, and blame the students: All of these are one-up messages on our part. Instead we encourage you to address consciously the following questions that will allow you to identify your own concern with this conflict. How do we communicate the purpose of our courses to our students? Are we unknowingly ignoring the "prerequisite" skills that students need to succeed in our classes? Do we assume that "some other part of the university" will teach the students to write, analyze, study, and so on? Do we assume little or no need or responsibility for relating our subject matter directly to our students' past, present, or future lives? In our departmental culture, what distinctions do we make between a course that emphasizes theory and one that emphasizes applications?

Available Strategies for the Professor. We can avoid the conflicts. We can ignore the indirect one-down messages that our students send when they fall asleep or are withdrawn or uninterested. When the question gets directly asked, we can one-up the student by answering in an abstract way such as: "All knowledge is ultimately practical," "That's for you to discover," "Knowledge deepens our understanding of the universe in which we live," "We just need to know this in order to understand what comes next," and so on. We can also choose to not take the time to question our own personal assumptions, read, think, or discuss with our colleagues the nature of this conflict. We can reinforce our status by complaining about our students to our colleagues.

Avoidance and its cousins, distraction and blame, temporarily displace the conflict for the professor. But these strategies often leave the student confused, put down, left out, and angry. These avoidance dynamics generate the heat that brings on hostility later.

We urge you to approach the conflict in a two-across manner that we believe creates the opportunity for learning and inclusion. Here are four suggestions.

1. Examine and challenge your own attitudes and beliefs about the purpose of education and the role of practicality. How do you feel about it? What is your struggle? Who has written on these issues?

2. Develop rhetorical and teaching strategies for relating to your students. Address the question directly and often: So why should you care about all this information? How will it help you? Figure out ways to get the students to struggle with the questions. Try as often as possible to use the experiences of the students as your starting point. Get the students to give you examples of how a particular theory relates to their experiences. Have oral and written assignments that demonstrate how the knowledge of a course can shed light on the issues or concerns of the students.

3. Be open, pay attention to the indirect relational messages that students may be sending you. Privately reach out to the students who appear to be withdrawing. In many instances what the student of color is looking for is just some visible sign that the professor cares about and is interested in his or her well-being.

4. Assess students' level of preparation for the course early in the term and then adapt your syllabus accordingly. We are all accustomed to evaluating students at the quarter or midpoint of the course and to sticking to our planned syllabus. For those students we consider underprepared, evaluations become punishments rather than opportunities to learn. As faculty members we must address why, when, and how we assess learning.

In short, all of these two-across strategies invite us to turn the classroom into the learning environment it was intended to be in which what the student brings is an important part of the process to be integrated with the professor's knowledge and lesson plans. Some would say these strategies are just good teaching regardless of the multicultural classroom. Yes, this is true. But in intercultural and interracial situations, when these strategies are consistently used, they send a clear and strong message that can deflate the perception of any other covert racial one-up messages that a faculty member may accidentally send. Students of color are a lot more likely to pay attention to two-across messages that reflect a professor's genuine concern for their well-being.

Available Strategies for the Student. Faculty members are not the only ones who need to address issues regarding the purpose of education. Students need to be encouraged to examine their own motives. They need to look beyond immediate job skills to the meaning of career. What potential does education offer them to increase their understanding of themselves as members of many interlocking communities, including their ethnic, gender, biological, psychological, professional, and regional communities? How can an education increase the quality of their family life, their community life, and their economic security? What does "quality of life" mean?

Moreover, students need to be encouraged to assess honestly their own academic skills. Being underprepared is no sin. Condemning yourself to always be so is. Asking the above questions should be a part of what faculty members bring to students regardless of their discipline. Get to know people in student services, counseling, and your academic skills center to whom you can refer students who need special help. Find out if a student needs help early in the semester or quarter and give him or her a referral in private. Do not disregard the student; continue to work with him or her. In many incidents you will see growth rather than the predictable failure.

Issues of Access and Affirmative Action

A European-American and an African-American professor prepare for a meeting in which affirmative action is on the agenda. Think about how the content and relational dynamics are likely to get played out in the meeting.

One European-American professor confided to a coauthor of this text who also is European-American:

> Since I came to the university five years ago there has been a big push to admit more minority students. Most of the ones who have been admitted to my department are African-American and Latino, with a few Asians. Some of them are doing all right, but most of them really don't have the academic preparation to do college work. The retention rate of these students is atrocious. Now we are being pressured to increase the minority enrollment in the graduate program by 20 percent. I just don't see how we can do it without lowering standards. I am not a racist, and I do believe we should do something for these people, but I just don't think it is right to put them in a situation where they are bound to fail. Also, I don't think it is fair to have them occupying slots that some more deserving students should have. I really do not know what, if anything, I will say at the meeting. I'm really not against affirmative action, but I don't think this is fair. We should just let in the best-qualified students.

The African-American professor, who is in a tenure track position, confides to an African-American coauthor of this text:

> Oh no! They are going to discuss affirmative action and minority students at the faculty meeting next week. I hate going to these meetings. Everybody is so stressed when we discuss affirmative action, and they keep looking at me. Every time I look up, someone is staring at me. I am not sure if they are waiting for me to say something or if they wish I would leave so they could really say what they want in their discussions. I can tell that they really are opposed to affirmative action. Some of them try to patronize me, always wanting to know my views.

They don't want to know my view on anything else, why this? Hell, I am a junior faculty member, they must know that I am afraid to tell them what I really think. Ah, that's it, they know that and they want me to tell them what they really want to hear. I'm just going to go to the meeting and sit there and say nothing. I hope I can do it. I hope one of those fools doesn't make me so angry that I really tell them what is on my mind. They are a pack of racists hiding behind the tired old slogan of "best qualified." When were any of them ever the best qualified for anything?

This situation is ripe for a divisive confrontation. Neither person wants to address the issue. If possible, both would like to avoid it. Neither shows a strong understanding of the content issues. However, both are keenly aware of the relational issues. The European-American professor sees himself as the keeper of the standard (Divider 2) and sees the students of color as the ones who must do all of the changing (Divider 7). If he does speak up, he is likely to do so from a one-up position. The African-American professor perceives these dividers in that others expect him to be the spokesperson for affirmative action issues (Divider 4). Moreover, the African-American faculty member's awkwardness with the issue and his low power in the department leave him believing that his only choices are to avoid the topic or lash out.

Recognizing Content Issues

Higher education is a scarce resource in society, so conflict over issues of access and affirmative action are inevitable. Every time we hire, fire, appoint, or retain people or make or implement policy of any kind we are in the affirmative action conflict, even if the topic is avoided. These issues are bitterly contested at schools across the nation, including the most elite ones. Access to universities for students of color is an admissions-standards conflict. Many who oppose affirmative action hold to Divider 5, which equates a change (letting students of color into the university) with lowering standards.

Still others believe in Divider 1: Race and gender do not and should not matter. On the other hand, some who advocate affirmative action and greater access for students of color use Connector 5 to say that Scholastic Aptitude Test (SAT) scores and grades are one, but not the only, way to measure who should get access to higher education. Others argue that taxpayer monies should not be used to support institutions that educate predominantly European-Americans when we are becoming a nation of many cultures. Those who advocate the maintenance of traditional standards begin to label and single out students of color as not being capable of meeting the admission standards of institutions of higher education. On the other side, affirmative action advocates are often guilty of labeling the gatekeepers of high standards as bigots and racists.

And so hard lines get drawn. The stakes and flames get even higher when we talk about finite resources in a depressed economy. There are only so many student slots and so much financial aid. To increase admissions for students of color means that fewer European-American students will gain entry and receive financial aid and special assistance.

Recognizing Relational Issues

The relational issue for faculty members and administrators who may view themselves as having lost positions or promotions because of an "affirmative action hire" generate animosity and a hardening of the belief that affirmative action lowers standards (Divider 5). This attitude is communicated to and felt by "affirmative action candidates." Students and faculty members of color can feel one-down because of the "affirmative action admit" label and undue pressure to "prove them wrong."

Available Strategies

Our two professors might be able to avoid having to talk about the issues at this particular meeting. However, by doing so they will support the status quo, which will perpetuate the current situation. Moreover, left unattended, conflicts around access and affirmative action can lead to the development of a false sense of superiority among European-Americans and a false sense of inferiority in people of color on our campuses. Pushed to the extreme, students and faculty of color are isolated, labeled, and treated as a pariah class. On the other hand, European-American students build up resentments, develop prejudices, and are often overtly hostile toward students of color. This is the stuff out of which racial incidents on campus are made.

We have a special responsibility to take the hysteria out of discussions about affirmative action and access. We must actively assist our students in better understanding the content and relational dynamics involved in affirmative action issues. We are not claiming to have the answers to affirmative action conflicts. However, we are certain that avoiding the issue is wrong and ineffective. So we now suggest seven ways in which to productively engage these issues.

1. Educate yourself about affirmative action. Read about it. Confront your own biases. Be willing to listen to others who are highly informed rather than just highly opinionated. Engage in regular discussions. Read articles and hold departmental and universitywide discussions.

2. Ponder these questions: How do we in education correct the current consequences of social and historical inequities within our colleges? What is our responsibility to educate a representative and proportional student body? What is our responsibility to provide a faculty that reflects the cultural diversity of our society?

3. Assess the inequities that exist on your campus. Look everywhere. Get students, faculty members, and staff members to share their perceptions of inequities.

4. Develop criteria for prioritizing the inequities.

5. Be willing to raise these issues in the classroom.

6. Address what is meant by "standards." How can affirmative action be used to raise the standards? Few have argued that balancing Harvard and Yale universities to effect geographic diversity has lowered their quality or standards. In fact, officials at these elite institutions will say that such diversity increases the quality of the university experience.

7. Institutionalize open discussions. Open discussions about access and affirmative action are helpful in dispelling rumors, half truths, and outright distortions about the intended purposes of such programs. In the final analysis, affirmative action is a good management tool. It ensures that the net is cast wide and that every effort is made to attract the brightest and best-qualified group of applicants. It is a mechanism that asks us to reexamine what we mean by "best qualified."

Freedom of Speech: Fighting Words

Whose fight? Whose words? Some faculty members feel victimized when their opposition to affirmative action or multicultural issues is labeled "racist." They retaliate with charges of "political correctness." Students demand the right to make racial jokes. Faculty members and students of color fear being labeled as hypersensitive, "PC police," and "too subjective" if they speak up about race issues. Well-intentioned faculty members, who want to teach from a more multicultural perspective fear the possible uproar and hostility that might occur if oppression and racism is or is not discussed. When the issue of race is present, students and faculty members alike worry about offending others or being jumped on. If the university is the free marketplace of ideas, then why are we having such a difficult time with discussions of race?

Content Issues

All too often, issues of race and freedom of speech are bogged down in whether any one individual has the legal right to make racist statements. Of course, the U.S. Constitution allows an individual the freedom to make all sorts of vile statements. However, if we stop our analysis here we are often paralyzed. We can label you as "racist," and you can label us as "PC police." So, what?

Let us suggest that as professors, most of us need not pretend to be lawyers or judges. Yes, we must abide by the First Amendment, and many of us must teach it. But as teachers we must also provide opportunities for students to understand and analyze the meaning and consequence of their attitudes and behaviors. We must teach students how to balance freedom of speech with the responsibility of speech.

Let us say that one of our biology faculty members is teaching as if DNA had not yet been discovered. Although this professor certainly has the individual and academic freedom to present such an argument, most of us would argue that it is irresponsible. When students make "mistakes" in understanding a theory, using a computation formula, identifying a period in history, or writing or speaking a language, we feel confident in "correcting" the error. When we are on our best behavior, we do so with sensitivity, seeing the mistake as an opportunity to teach. We pave the way for the student to awaken to his or her own error. Freedom of speech issues are the last thing on our mind. Yet when students or faculty members want to affirm racial superiority, monocultural or multicultural approaches to education, affirmative action, and so on, then freedom of speech becomes the one and only issue that some people think about.

It is no accident that freedom of speech issues on campus are most often racial issues. We contend that not taking a stand on racial issues is to perpetuate racism.

Relational Issues

The relational message that often gets communicated is that the individual's right to use racist language is always more important than any social or relational responsibility to communicate messages that contribute to a common good and to reflect social reality accurately. These relational messages constrict the dialogue by denying the feelings of the individuals and the communities involved. They are one-up messages that attempt to control, limit, and shut down debate and discussion.

The beating of an African-American, Rodney King, by a gang of European-American policemen in Los Angeles, California, and their acquittal on charges of assault brought a period of both stress and great opportunity on our college campuses. Many European-American students (and faculty members, for that matter) were facing the awareness of being white for the first time. "I have never felt so white before." "I have never felt so ashamed of my people before." "I am afraid to look black students in the eye." "I am afraid they want to take their anger out on me." Many students and faculty members of color were enraged and pulled out of whatever complacency they were in. They knew that those police officers could just as easily have savagely beat them, their children, other family members, and friends. The stage was set for trouble.

Available Strategies for Faculty and Administrators

Many faculty and administrators wanted to avoid the situation by quickly denouncing the Rodney King verdict as wrong and as an isolated incident of racism while at the same time denouncing the disturbances in South-Central Los Angeles as "understandable but inappropriate." But many of these faculty members and administrators then went on with "business as usual." Such a strategy works as a one-up message: "I will control and judge what is important to talk about." Faculty members denied class time to discuss students' feelings and experiences with the situation. Administrators vetoed permission for open-microphone or protest forums. Some students complied; although the strategy worked in the short run, the learning opportunity was lost. However, on many campuses across the country, especially in California, faculty members and administrators who tried these avoidance strategies found students walking out of their classrooms. Other students disrupted their classes and went on to participate in unruly protests to vent their anger and confusion.

One campus in particular chose a two-across strategy that included having the school newspaper run several articles on the incident and encouraging students to write letters to the editor. Faculty members in several departments (such as health sciences, ethnic studies, human development, speech communication, chemistry, and criminal justice) used the incident as the backdrop for lectures on such subjects as racism, oppression, environmental issues, police practices in minority communities, inequality, identity, and social policy. These lectures and discussions provided students with the opportunity to see members of the academic community discussing issues of racism and police brutality in the context of their disciplines. The faculty members were able to provide the intellectual and theoretical grounding for the students to frame their feelings and experiences.

On another campus administrators assisted and encouraged an open-microphone session in which students and faculty members discussed their views and feelings on the verdict and the resulting unrest. During the open-mike speeches, many students of color spoke of the daily indignities and anger of living in a white racist society. Many European-American students spoke of wanting everybody to "just get along." Students and faculty of color responded by telling the European-American students to "get real" and acknowledge the racial divide. The institution's president, a European-American female, spoke of her own pain and confusion over the situation and her pride in the students for their civil openness. Many harsh statements were made, and tears fell. However, because the forum was committed to understanding one another's experiences, it served to bridge the very divide it exposed.

At the same campus, many of the students and faculty members who attended the open-mike session participated in a spontaneous march against racism the next day. These two events, with the participation of faculty members, students, and administrators of all ethnicities helped to create a sense of community out of one of the most potentially divisive incidents in many years.

Many of our campuses are incidents waiting to happen. Racial jokes on campus radio stations, slave auctions, and racial slurs on posters and walls all set the stage for conflict and disorder. How can we approach these incidents as both opportunities and teaching moments?

1. Gather all of the facts surrounding an incident. Try not to deal with hearsay and rumors.
2. Meet with all parties involved as quickly as possible. Initially, it is a good idea to meet with the groups separately.
3. Faculty members and administrators in the academic community who have expertise in race relations should be involved if negotiations and mediation are needed.
4. Explore with both sides what they would consider to be appropriate resolutions to the conflict.

These actions can be particularly effective if European-American faculty and staff members have long-term, two-across working relations with their counterparts among faculty and staff members of color. Their "community" and working together will be an example to students.

For all race-related situations, we suggest that faculty members take the following steps:

1. Discuss both the content and the relational dynamics of the situation.
2. Discuss the context that grows and breeds such behavior.
3. Provide factual and theoretical frames for helping students understand the historical and current dynamics that perpetuate such behaviors.
4. If you are uncomfortable leading such discussions, invite someone on your campus to be a guest leader.

5. Encourage students to do assignments that assess the course theories and concepts for their utility to address racial issues.
6. Engage other faculty members and administrators in discussions dealing with race relations.

Ethnic Studies and Multicultural Education

Just about everyone we know has a favorite ethnic studies story. Although some are about its value and benefits for students, the university, and the community, all too often we hear horror stories. "Those ethnic studies programs are a waste of time." "They are just giving away grades over there and lowering the standards of this university." "We do not need ethnic studies. The students cannot find jobs, and no graduate school will accept graduates of such programs, anyway. Besides, if we integrate multicultural perspectives into the curriculum, we will not need ethnic studies." Although most of those who spread such rumors do not stop to verify their accusations, it does not stop such tales from growing and becoming tacit assumptions upon which hostile conflicts are built.

A Conflict

The political science department recruits and hires an African-American professor. His specialty is the politics of the African-American community. He and the department want him to teach the course in the political science department despite the fact that a similar course is already being offered in the ethnic studies department. The ethnic studies department chair and faculty complain, the African-American student union gets involved, and a major conflict develops.

Identifying Content Issues

Ethnic studies programs and departments grew out of the student protests and conflicts of the 1960s. There has been a historical strain between these programs and the rest of the university community, one that persists to this day. Some traditionalists in the academic community tend to see ethnic studies as the unwelcome intruder, the pretender to academic credibility. Some ethnic studies proponents see the traditional university as out to get them, as vultures and racists out to destroy them.

In this particular case, ethnic studies used the academic senate's established policy against course duplication to argue that a course titled "The African-American Community" is already being taught in ethnic studies. And given tough budget times, our academic resources had to be managed carefully. Political science faculty members quickly counter by saying that they have the right to teach the course and that any attempt to prevent them from doing so is a violation of their academic freedom. The administration sides with political science.

Although this conflict is quite complex and has many tributaries, we will highlight three major content questions.

1. As more traditional departments integrate multicultural perspectives and develop multicultural courses, how should colleges handle the duplication or similarity of courses? How is the issue one of academic freedom and departmental autonomy?
2. What is the role, position, and status of the ethnic studies department in the university?
3. Is the movement to "mainstream" multicultural perspectives seen as an alternative or as an addition to the ethnic studies department? In short, is it a thinly veiled attempt to abolish ethnic studies?

Identifying the Relational Issues

Ethnic studies programs, especially the one in this case, have been continually on trial. Faculty members and their courses and scholarship are held in contempt. Ethnic studies faculty members have good reasons to fear that the "multicultural movement" is being used to cut the program. The African-American political scientist's insistence on teaching the topic with the backing of his department can be interpreted by the rest of the university as a relational message that the political science department is more legitimate than ethnic studies. Moreover, by ignoring the academic senate ruling, the administration supports the one-down relational message to ethnic studies and further marginalizes its faculty and supporters. This marginalization leads ethnic studies faculty members to live in fear that their program will be cut or abolished. Thus every conflict becomes a confrontation over academic survival.

Available Strategies for Nonethnic Studies Faculty and Administrators. To avoid the issue is to support the status quo on your campus. If ethnic studies is ghettoized and ignored, then it will slowly deteriorate. If ethnic studies is not consulted and treated as a major player or if you do not have an ethnic studies program and you avoid discussing its absence, then you sideline yourself in an exciting transitional phase in higher education. If you avoid raising the issues of standards for instituting new courses, departmental autonomy, and courses, then you perpetuate the status quo.

Here are some strategies for approaching the ethnic studies issue in a two-across manner.

1. Let the ethnic studies department know that you are hiring an African-American faculty member who has expertise in an area that may duplicate the course offerings in ethnic studies. Discuss the department's perspectives on the role of ethnic studies and multicultural issues. Explore the possibility of cross-listing courses. Be open to hearing the department's concerns.
2. Examine your own attitudes and knowledge about ethnic studies.
3. Begin to raise the issue of the role of ethnic studies as we move into teaching from a more multicultural perspective.

4. Begin to read ethnic studies scholarship in your field. Remember that there is only one ethnic studies doctoral program in the United States. Almost all of our ethnic studies faculty members received their doctorates in traditional fields. Their research and scholarship often reflect their discipline training although they most often publish in ethnic studies journals.

5. Explore the possibility of having the new faculty member teach some courses in the ethnic studies department.

6. Try on the idea of looking at ethnic studies and multicultural education much the way you would the English department and writing across the curriculum. Just because we think all students need to know how to write well in all classes does not mean we are ready to consider dismantling English departments. Similarly, just because we are beginning to integrate multicultural perspectives across the curriculum does not mean that we should dismantle ethnic studies. Instead, both English and ethnic studies can be viewed as resources on which we must draw.

Summary

As our colleges and universities become increasingly diverse culturally and racially, we need to intensify our efforts to find better ways to include those who have been excluded for too long. We have a special role to play in developing strategies and finding solutions to intercultural and interracial conflicts. Teaching has never been easy. But when intercultural and interracial conflicts erupt on our campuses, it makes our task even more difficult. We must make friends with these increased conflicts. Only then will we get better at transforming these challenges into opportunities. We become more interculturally competent when we truly see people of color as our equal partners on the path of education. Together we must continue to experiment; we must continue to try to be more inclusive and to become increasingly more comfortable in working through the discomforts of intercultural and interracial conflicts. (See Chart 4.1.)

Chart 4.1 Engaging Race-Related Conflicts

---

1. Conflict is inevitable!
2. Avoiding intercultural conflicts and blaming, ignoring, and belittling others or the issues is unproductive and divisive.
3. Attempt to approach interracial conflicts in a two-across manner.
4. Analyze and attend to the content and relational issues and cues from all sides.
5. Examine your own feelings, beliefs, and knowledge.
6. Encourage the exposure of all agendas, including your own.
7. Examine the relationship between individual conflict and institutional inequities.
8. Be willing to raise difficult and unpopular issues in public and do so with racial connectors.
9. Use political networks both inside and outside the college to address the issue.
10. Institutionalize open discussions about current and potential race-related conflicts.

The next chapter draws together the implications of racial identity, the myths of race, the need to better communicate, and the creative use of conflict.

5 | Toward New Racial and Cultural Boundaries in the Academy

One cannot become more skilled at interpersonal and intercultural communications, conflict resolution, and social interactions as a matter of good public-image making. Although we have suggested a variety of paths you can pursue to improve outcomes for your students, college, and yourself, it should be clear that there is no shortcut to becoming skilled and expert at interracial and intercultural relations overnight. It takes personal effort and practice to become a communications connector rather than a divider and to be able to see conflicts as opportunities for mutual learning and resolution.

However, let us now suggest two of the more difficult challenges we face as academics: (a) How can we as individuals question and break from the historic constraints of race to see races as what they really are—communities of interest? (b) How can we contribute to the institutional changes that will transform our colleges into truly inclusive learning communities?

Communities of Interest Defined

European-Americans, African-Americans, Latinos and Latinas, Native Americans, and Asian-Americans are considered to be racial groups when in fact they are much more historic communities of interests. By referring, for example, to all people of European descent as "white people" or even as "European-Americans," we ignore the very real diversity of cultures and circumstances among peoples of European descent in the United States.

Focusing on a community of interests helps us to answer this question: Who has intergenerational advantages? Specifically, descendants of early English, German, and other settlers from northern Europe are a minority of the nation's population and a minority even among European-Americans. Yet they are vastly overrepresented and clearly dominate business and government leaders as corporate board members, investors, upper-level corporate executives, U.S. senators, presidents, faculty members and administrators at prestigious universities, senior military officers, judges, legislators, and other state and federal directors and chief executives. The consistent intergenerational dominance that this powerful northern European-American minority enjoys is due to its noncompetitive advantages being defended by the majority of Europeans of other national cultural backgrounds as part of a general "white interest."

The vast majority of European-Americans are willing to overlook long-term group inequality among themselves for the privilege of being racially superior and having long-term advantages over nonwhites. If a general white racial community of interest did not exist, we would have to deal with our ethnic cultural differences, which are in fact the major barrier to leveling the playing field for individual achievement and talent to emerge, regardless of race or cultural background.

African-Americans, Native-Americans, Latinos, and Asian-Americans also constitute communities of interest who work hard to cultivate and maintain racial consciousness in order to advance their collective interests. To a significant degree, communities of interest among people of color have been based on reactions to racism, power dominance, and other forms of oppression perpetuated by European-Americans.

The end result is that we are a nation and academy of competing racial communities of interests. But there is, in fact, no real competition because our organization of interests by historic physical races obscures the very real built-in advantages of a cultural minority of old-line northern Europeans. Moreover, when other communities of interest resist or fail to conform to the dominant community of interests, then they are often perceived as deviant or pathological when, in fact, they are often legitimately calling for recognition as distinct communities of interest. Finally, the irony of racial communities of interests is that membership and assumed allegiance is determined by birth and is fixed by physical appearance.

Redefining Communities of Interests

What is the role of educators and the college community in dealing with racial communities of interests? We must work toward making the university a forum for uncovering, defining, studying, and analyzing these racial communities of interest.

There is a need to explore and understand the underlying cultural and circumstantial diversity within each so-called race. Clearly, everyone within the university, whether faculty member or student and regardless of discipline, needs to understand that racial differences are cultural and circumstantial, not biological. We need to also understand the role of physical racial identification in obscuring the real cultural differences within and between the races. We need to also understand how race plays a historically conditioned role by setting up no-win racial communities of interests and that racial communities of interests virtually guarantee continued inequality for most Americans, including most whites.

Knowledge of the myth of physical race and the self-limiting role of racial communities of interests should be central to the definition of an educated person. It will allow students, faculty members, and staff members of all ethnicities to realize that they can decide and define for themselves what role they will play, if any, in their racial communities of interest. Moreover, each of us becomes responsible for examining and redefining our own community of interest in such a way as to nurture our own ethnic identity while also discovering ways to contribute to an inclusive education community. Such knowledge might also result in efforts to redefine and organize alternative communities of interest. More of us in the academy might come to realize the extent to which the formal and informal organization of the college has been used to play out racial competition and reflect the interests of not only white Americans, but also a minority even among whites.

Instead, the college should be its own community of interest; that interest should be the pursuit of knowledge and the improvement of the larger society across all ethnic and historic identities. Most colleges claim this noble goal, but in reality a very select part of one people's culture, history, and development dominates higher education in the United States. All other people's cultures and experiences in either domestic or foreign histories and contemporary society are electives and of peripheral importance.

Identity Setting and Managing Expectations

If we want to be successful and productive in the multicultural college community, we must recognize that it will require hard work and a willingness to experiment and even make mistakes. A good starting point is to become skilled at reading racial messages and resolving crossracial and cultural conflicts. This requires our conscious participation each and every time we communicate and take action. In intercultural and interracial interactions we often have a range of choices that are not commonly explored. As a participant in any community, we must work toward enriching and expanding that community of interests to include the necessary ethnic-specific interests as well as the common interests and goals of other communities of interest. Faculty members and students of color should not have to be all things to all people as part of fulfilling commitments to their own racial communities of interest. Nor should they have to be compelled to ignore their historic communities and align themselves with white communities of interest in order to succeed in higher education. In the same way, it should not be the assumed privilege and responsibility of European-Americans to define and control all that is significant in higher education.

It is important to be clear, knowledgeable, and critical of one's specific cultural identity, whether it is historic, adopted, or multiple. Our ethnic and cultural identity is much closer to who we are than is some overall racial identity. It is also important to know what communities of interest we support or oppose and why. This form of self-knowledge and clarity is important not only for academic or ethical reasons, but also because it is the basis of defining and discovering our unique and individual contributions, interests, and purposes.

Understanding our cultural and ethnic identity is neither static nor easy. We live in a state of constant tension between our own ethnic- and race-specific communities of interest and an emerging community of interest for the common good. This tension is inevitable and, although it can be acknowledged or ignored and used as either a creative or destructive force, its consequences are inevitable.

Learning to communicate and resolve social conflicts between racial communities of interest necessitates tapping into our inner racial and ethnic identity as they relate to our professional interests and motivations. It is unlikely that we will be able to distinguish our personal convictions from social conditioning if we are unclear about our own social identity and community allegiances. We are in a unique position once we are clear about our cultural identity and communities of interest and have a well-developed sense of our personal interests and motivation. We can see the choices and actively work toward creating more desirable circumstance for ourselves and others by learning and then negotiating the expectations that colleagues and superiors have of us.

A note of caution. Yes, redefining our communities of interest to include our participation in both our ethnic-specific community and a new inclusive educational community is necessary for all of us. However, because of the historic and present-day role of European-Americans in excluding people of color from educational institutions, a particular burden is placed on those of us who are European-American. Those of us who are people of color have less power in this society and in education than do European-Americans, but we are not powerless and cannot be excused from working to break down the barriers that exclude us.

Using the Communities-of-Interest Concept in the College

Recognizing that the college, the classroom, the student union, and even the hometown are living spaces of various communities of interest, let us take another look at some of the examples from previous chapters to demonstrate how the communities-of-interest concept enlarges our understanding of the diversity issues on our campuses.

Communities of Interest and Unwritten Rules

In Chapter 1, Maria T., the Latina professor who is on a tenure track, has "membership" in at least three communities of interest: Latino (racial and ethnic-specific), female (gender), and traditional European-American-dominated higher education. Each community of interests has varying levels of visibility, power, and influence on Maria and on her department and college. The most powerful and the one considered the most legitimate by institutional standards is the European-American-dominated college culture. Personally, however, Maria T. feels a strong pull toward her specific ethnic and racial community of interest, including the women within her ethnic community. These two communities of interest intersect to give Maria a strong sense of loyalty to her ethnic and gender communities of interest, and they serve as a vital force in her professional life.

Each community of interests has its own set of unwritten tenets. When those unwritten rules remain unexamined, they are likely to erupt in a conflict in which the dominant community of interest wins out by excluding the others. Such was the case for Maria T. She needed to examine consciously the unwritten rules of each community of interest and identify potential areas of conflict for herself personally and professionally. If necessary, she would have to redefine her communities of interests so that she could work with students of color while also obtaining tenure. In short, Maria needed senior faculty members within the education community of interest to become committed and supportive of her research and publication plans, her teaching, her advising, and her community work. Moreover, she also needed support from members of her ethnic and racial community of interest. By first exposing, analyzing, and then redefining her personal and professional identities and goals, Maria T. might have been able to negotiate more successfully the inevitable conflicts between and among these communities of interest.

Communities of Interest and the Myths and Realities of Racism

The communities-of-interest concept is especially helpful in examining the myths and realities of racism. It allows us to question how community perpetuates and has a stake in one or more of the myths of racism and racial identity. Once we identify our communities of interest, we can begin to understand how we use and communicate the myths to overtly or covertly protect our communities of interest.

For example, say we follow our own advice from Chapter 2 and assess our grade distribution based on race; say we discover that the grades *are* race-stratified, with European-Americans getting the best grades. Ouch! Regardless of our intentions, this *is* a failure to educate. Moreover, we have perpetuated many of the myths of racism, especially the one that race determines aptitude and talent, and in so doing contributed to such stereotypes as blacks are lazy, Latinos are not as intelligent, and so on. By perpetuating these myths, we have also protected the European-American-dominated community of interest. When our department gets involved in hiring decisions, myths around race and affirmative action run rampant. If we become uncomfortable and avoid discussing the need for diversity hiring, hide behind code words, or passively allow others to passively search for "qualified minority" candidates, then we are protecting the European-American-dominated community of interest from including others.

By unmasking the myths of racism in terms of their influence on the relevant communities of interest, we can see how they serve to protect and exclude. The onus is on all of us to redefine our community of interest so that it is more inclusive. Even though it is disquieting, we recognize that it is far safer to contemplate privately the influence of the myths and realities of racism on one's own communities of interest than to commit to examine publicly and professionally the unwritten rules and myths of racism that we, our colleagues, and superiors are perpetuating.

In Chapter 3, however, we suggested that these difficult topics can be communicated in a way that invites analysis, cooperation, and change.

Communicating About Communities of Interest

Professor Lincoln, the elegant writer who prides himself on teaching diverse students how to write well, had a clear sense of his personal self-direction. He was doing what he enjoyed and had some success. But his success was based on students conforming to his intellectual and professional standards as well as his cultural community of interest. Students of color were successful with him if, in effect, they became "honorary whites"—that is, elegant writers of the English language as defined by Lincoln.

Joyce, the African-American student in Lincoln's class, had a sense of her ethnic and racial community of interest and also wanted to be accepted as a member in the academy. She perceived that Lincoln was both a threat to her ethnic and racial community of interest and a ticket to the academic community of interest. Moreover, she clearly viewed the academic community of interest as an exclusive European-American-dominated community. Both Lincoln and Joyce need to fully expose, critique, and define their own racial and ethnic-specific communities of interest and their relationship to the current and potentially inclusive academic community. Lincoln needs to decide if he is going to continue to protect only the European-American community of interest or if he is going to discover ways to make the academic community one that is truly a common community.

Like all of us, Professor Lincoln makes mistakes and unintentionally offends others and protects his own community of interest in an exclusionary way. However, we all have a choice. Major conflicts in the college community begin with an accumulation of unresolved one-on-one offenses in which the offenders are clueless to the misery they have caused others until a major public conflict arises. We recommend one-on-one resolution of personal and cultural offenses as soon as possible after the offense. We also recommend public discussion of how to create an educational community of interest that is characterized by a common educational community that is not dominated by any one specific ethnic and cultural community.

Conflicting Communities of Interest

The conflicts highlighted in Chapter 4 could have benefited from such an overarching mission. The case study involving the ethnic studies and the political science departments illustrates our point. There are three competing communities of interests:

1. the traditional European-American educational community in the form of the administrators and the political science department, with a single African-American course offering being taught by an African-American;
2. the ethnic studies community of interest being put in the position of representing all non-European-American communities of interest; and
3. the students representing all of the ethnic and racial communities of interest.

The administrators, political science faculty, and ethnic studies faculty should have agreed to expose, analyze, and redefine each community of interest involved in the conflict. The purpose would then be to develop a policy and practice that reflect the ethnic-specific communities of interest as well as an inclusive educational community of interest that is not dominated by any one ethnic community of interest. Then we might have seen a far more creative solution. As it was, the dominant community of interest won, and a grand opportunity was lost.

The Role of the Institution

Cooperatively confronting and communicating about race-related conflicts is just not possible unless all of us critically examine and redefine our cultural identity and our role in excluding those who are perceived as different from us—especially those of us who are European-Americans. We harbor a sense of racial superiority that results in the so-called benign isolation and friendly rejection of colleagues and students of color. We have the greatest need to examine critically and redefine our cultural identity, become clear about our communities of interest, and be in touch with our personal motivations and interests. Many of us will be able to immediately see through our historic conditioning. Some of us are more likely to become interested and curious about what is really going on in the minds and hearts of other European-Americans and people of color around us. Still others will continue to act out a "them versus us" worldview, although they may better understand why they are doing it. In the long run, the college community will be better for it and so will the nation.

Although there is much we can do as individual faculty members and administrators to make the college a more inclusive place and to teach from a more multicultural perspective, we must recognize the power and intransigence of the institutions of higher education in which we labor. In short, there is an institutional responsibility that has to be activated. Some faculty members, for whatever reason, will not change and, given the enormous autonomy we exercise, this places even more pressure on the institutional response.

There are people who will not develop a more critical awareness of who they are with regard to race and culture. They are simply not going to change on their own. They need tenure, the classroom, and the status quo to lord over colleagues and students alike. They want to work only with students who come to them as the "very best," already educated and thoroughly European-American as an honorary or factual ascription. Any difference in a condition is simply not good enough, especially if the students are of different colors and cultures. Are these faculty members hopeless? Hardly. They also can change, but for them the motive will have to be self-interest.

How can we effect this? We can do two things:

1. We can make certain that the formal and informal institutional criteria for evaluating faculty and teaching assistants include excellence in multicultural curriculum development and teaching and working with multicultural and multiracial students.
2. We can then make certain that faculty members are held accountable to these important additional criteria for excellence.

We are talking here about institutionalizing the commitment to diversity in such a way that it impacts every aspect of determining who gets hired, retained, and promoted. They will see the light or have to find something else to do.

Models of Success

A lot has been said in previous chapters, and a lot of advice has been offered. If we put all of the challenges for new skills and competencies on the table, what would they look like and what would people who have them look like? Chart 5.1 matches competencies with questions that one would explore to arrive at each competency. Note that each competency comes out of discussions in this and the preceding chapters. Also, these are not perceived competencies or intended competencies, they are day-to-day, action-oriented competencies. The chart is followed by examples of people who embody them.

We now describe people who have modeled these competencies, inspired us, and invigorated their own and all our lives and professions.

David B. is a European-American English instructor who teaches a required course in English literature and writing to a highly diverse freshman class. The class is diverse in background preparation, writing skills, racial and ethnic backgrounds, and social class. David's other colleagues, who also teach this class, routinely fail or discourage most of the students of color by the end of the semester. Their classes are tense and account for a good deal of the attrition among freshman students of color from the college.

Walk by David B.'s colleagues' classes, and the students are quietly listening to lectures. Walk by David's class and there is animated discussion, occasional laughter, and some quiet intense moments. David's class is clearly different, and outcomes for European-American and students of color alike are different. Everyone is challenged, everyone improves his or her appreciation for literature and writing skills and learns a great deal from and about one another. European-American and students of color advise one another to take David's over all others, including the department's instructor of color. Finally, David's class does not simply end. His students regularly give him cards of appreciation with their signatures, and they take class pictures on the last day.

Chart 5.1 A Review of Competencies

Competencies	Framework for Analysis
1. Know and be critical of your own ethnic identity. Be who you are!	1. What are the ethnic-identity issues and social context?
2. Expose and share your department's unwritten rules and contexts.	2. What are the unwritten rules? How do they influence people of color and European-Americans? What is the context for understanding these rules?
3. Your individual actions represent and support the institutional goals for diversity.	3. How do individual decisions and actions support and resist the institution's goals of diversity?
4. Openly acknowledge and discuss the myths and realities of racism.	4. What are the operating myths and realities of racism in each situation and throughout your institution in general?
5. Speak and listen with conscious awareness for both the content and relational racial and cultural messages being sent and received.	5. What are the content and relational racial dynamics?
6. Communicate two-across connecting messages that honor your own and the other's perspective. Work to establish win-win, inclusive understandings and solutions.	6. What are the types of one-up and one-down dividing messages and two-across connecting messages that get communicated? By whom are they communicated?
7. View interracial and diversity-related conflicts as opportunities to approach and creatively engage people in confronting significant issues.	7. How and what interracial and diversity-related conflicts are avoided? approached? What are the content and relational issues?
8. Believe and communicate that education is a community of interest that includes many communities of interest.	8. What are the ethnic and other specific communities of interest? Where is there tension? Is it potentially healthy and necessary or is it harmful? Can it be alleviated?

David B. has had years of experience interacting with other European-Americans and students of color in many different settings, and with upper-class, working-class, and blue-collar people of all political and cultural persuasions. He has worked in youth homes and was a Peace Corps volunteer in Africa. He is skilled at connective communications and two-across interactions. He is also skilled at resolving racial and cultural conflicts, and he uses conflict in his teaching. To David, education is not simply teaching English literature and writing, it is for each student to learn English literature and written expression from one another's experiences: their own and others'. The academic exercise and objectives are never separated in his class from the individuals' experiences as a basis of critical reading and effective writing. David also has close friends of other cultural backgrounds with whom he has learned, disclosed, argued, debated, and experienced things in common.

Jim C. is a European-American graduate student with a strong interest in theory. He is routinely the top student in his department's graduate seminars. His analyses of various theories are insightful and penetrating, and his critiques are devastating. Faculty members respect his intellect and have learned a great deal from having Jim in their classes. Several have sought Jim out as a co-writer for professional journal articles. Unlike other senior graduate students, Jim is very close to the students of color in his department. Some students and faculty alike have wondered why someone so brilliant and theoretical finds the struggling students of color interesting. They have concluded that this is part of Jim's eccentricity.

Not only is Jim C. close to the graduate students of color in his department, but also they accept him, and not because he is eccentric. He recognizes how the other European-American students and faculty see them. He has routinely provided his peers of color with invaluable guidance, insight, and information that has helped them to deal successfully with and survive in the department. Jim's peers of color see and feel his recognition of their intellectual merit and the academic potential of their experiences, points of view, and impressions of the mainstream theory and methods in their field of study.

Jim C. and several of his graduate peers of color have been part of a now-famous play on racism in their department and in journal evaluations of articles. Jim wrote a paper for the department journal but submitted it under an African-American student's name. The article was rejected. The same African-American student wrote a paper and submitted it under Jim's name. It was published. Then both students wrote an article about racism and labeling using both article submissions as case studies. Jim arrived at his very deep conviction about equity by being open and willing to learn from people of other races and social classes. He has been known to talk with gas station attendants and people on the streets for hours, and he claims to learn much from them. This is how he learned to be a two-across communicator.

Pearl D. is an African-American woman who teaches African-American and African history. The African-American students in her university struggled to get a faculty member of color who could teach this very important course. The students who took her course on African history expected the focus to be exclusively on Africa. They were surprised to find that it was also necessary to study aspects of European and Middle Eastern history in order to understand developments in Africa. At first they were resistant, but then they began to see that African and European histories were interrelated and that it would be difficult if not impossible to understand developments and events in one place without also having a sense of developments and events in the other.

Pearl D. is passionate about who she is and what she does. Ever since she was an undergraduate she has not let herself or her friends isolate her from interactions with other people. Her reaction was one of curiosity to people who were different or who saw her as only a black woman and a subordinate. She would walk up to them, talk with them, and challenge them to find out how they thought and why they held the views they did. As part of her training in African history, she insisted on traveling not only in Africa, but also in Europe. She has the same view of teaching African-American history:

It is not a history apart from general American history. An American history that does not deal with Native Americans and Africans from their experiences is only a history of Europeans in America and from a European point of view. In fact, both African-American and American history are much broader and richer when they include the developments and events of Europeans as well as peoples of color.

Mac S. is a European-American dean of a college. He has a passion for travel in Europe and good opera. Under his leadership, enrollments in the humanities and social sciences increased despite a downward national trend. His college has very successfully recruited and retained top-caliber faculty members of color and has several innovative teaching and interdisciplinary programs. The dean is well respected by senior central administrators and faculty members alike. What is unusual about Mac is that he is also seen as a leader among students and faculty of color. They regularly seek his advice and counsel on issues and trust his judgment and fairness. He has both supported advocates of color against faculty opposition on issues he believed to be correct and has opposed them even when they have had faculty support if he felt that they were wrong. When faculty members have dragged their feet on issues affecting people of color, the dean is one of the first to call for action.

Mac S. is a careful listener. He is interested in not only what someone says but also what he or she means to say, as well as what he or she is reluctant to say. He extends trust and expects it in return. Mac has none of the insecurities associated with people who are fearful or threatened by others who are different. Whether he agrees with you or not, the basis of his decisions and reaction to you is out of a basic principle of fairness tempered by his amazing ability as a listener.

These cases are indeed of extraordinary and well-grounded people. But how they became extraordinary is no secret or accident of birth. So what do these four people have in common? They are not all liberals or conservatives. They are not all European-Americans or people of color. They are not in the same disciplines. They are faculty members, a graduate student, and a dean. So what *do* they have in common?

First, they are all culturally and personally authentic. In affirming their own cultural backgrounds, they do not find it necessary to oppose others. They do not have the need to reject their own cultures to affirm another. They clearly enjoy what they do, are highly motivated in doing it, and are professionally very effective. Second, as scholars, graduate student, and administrator, they affirm their own communities of interest, but they do so without defining them singularly or narrowly. They all believe that it is positive for people of all communities to be educated about their own histories and background and that one people's experiences cannot be separated from the others. Education is learning about oneself and others. Finally, they are all committed to the ideal that the university is a positive, a win-win community of interest.

The most enjoyable learning, the finest creative art, the most skillful management, and the most inspiring teaching come out of deep personal curiosity, interests, motivation, and conviction. It is as if they all have some special mission or purpose to their lives. This inner sense of self and direction could not be fully realized if their social identities were obscured.

All of these people had learned to see themselves and others through the eyes of all the different people to whom they related, whether or not the others were from their own racial, ethnic, and social class backgrounds. This common skill and competency gives them an extraordinary window onto their own taken-for-granted, assumed, and unconscious assumptions about themselves and others. They are each experienced in effective communications across domestic cultural barriers and have benefited from the higher degree of self-disclosure and self-knowledge such communications requires in comparison to the limited communications within one's immediate cultural group.

What these people have achieved is not unique and does not require extraordinary talent or a special personality. Each comes to improving his or her intercultural communications in a unique way. To become as effective as they are requires effort over time, plus trial and error. If we do the same, there will be mistakes, but there will also be learning. The end result will be a richer and more vigorous intellectual, personal, and professional life—and a better university.

In conclusion, it has never been an easy task to teach in our colleges and universities. Our ever-increasing ethnic and racial diversity has made it even more difficult. Instead of ignoring this fact or blaming the students for not being "as good as they used to be," we should all honestly and deeply critique our role as educators in the 21st century. Step forward and wrestle with the tough questions, new and old, of how to better prepare our students for an ever-changing society. In some cases we ask you to make a paradigm shift, and in all cases we ask that you look beneath the surface of your own layers of institutional policy and Eurocentric socialization and ferret out those attitudes, traditions, and behaviors that alienate and exclude so many of our students and faculty members of color.

We hope you will be an active participant in the struggle to make our colleges more inclusive. These are exciting, rough, and unstable times that are not unlike the civil rights years of the 1960s. If all of the folks who now say they participated in that struggle back then actually had, then we would be much farther along today. Now we have another chance. We can choose to sit in our armchairs and lie to our grandchildren when they ask "Where were you when the great educational movement of the 1990s happened?" Or we can tell them honestly the stories of the personal challenges and the insecurities we faced, the mistakes we made, and the victories we won when we participated in creating changes that mattered.

Selected References and Suggested Readings

Altbach, P. G., & Lomotey, K. (Eds.). (1991). *The racial crisis in American higher education*. Albany: State University of New York Press.

Anzaldua, G. (1990). Haciendo caras, una entrada. In G. Anzaldua (Ed.), *Making face, making soul haciendo caras* (pp. xv-xxvii). San Francisco: Aunt Lute Foundation.

Asante, M. (1987). *The Afrocentric idea*. Philadelphia: Temple University Press.

Auletta, G., & Jones, T. (1990). Reconstituting the inner circle. *American Behavioral Scientist, 34*(2), 137-152.

Auletta, G. S., & Jones, T. (in press). Unmasking the myths of racism in the classroom. In D. Halpern (Ed.), *Changing college classrooms: The challenge of educating students for the 21st century*. San Francisco: Jossey Bass.

Auletta, G. S., & Jones, T. (Eds.). (1990). The inclusive university: Multicultural perspectives in higher education [Special issue]. *American Behavioral Scientist, 34*(2).

Banks, J. (1976). *The sociology of education*. New York: Schocken.

Banks, J. (1991). Multicultural literacy and curriculum reform. *Education Digest, 57*, 10-13.

Bannister, R. C. (1979). *Social Darwinism: Science and myth in Anglo-American social thought*. Philadelphia: Temple University Press.

Banton, M. (1988). *Racial consciousness*. New York: Longman.

Bennett, L. (1965). Miscegenation in America. In C. M. Larson (Ed.), *Marriage across the color line*. Chicago: Johnson.

Berry, W. (1989). *The hidden wound*. San Francisco: North Point Press.

Blauner, R. (1972). *Racial oppression in America*. New York: Harper & Row.

Blauner, R. (1989). *Black lives, white lives: Three decades of race relations in America*. Berkeley: University of California Press.

Bourdieu, P., & Passeron, J. C. (1990). *Reproduction in education, society and culture.* Newbury Park, CA: Sage.

Bowser, B. P. (1985). Race relations in the 1980s: The case of the U.S. *Journal of Black Studies, 15*(3), 304-324.

Bowser, B. P. (1986). Community and economic context of black families: A critical review of the literature. *The American Journal of Social Psychiatry, 6*(1), 17-26.

Bowser, B. P. (Ed.). (1991). *Black male adolescents: Parenting and education in community context.* Lanham, MD: University Press of America.

Bowser, B. P., & Hunt, R. G. (Eds.). (1981). *Impacts of racism on white Americans.* Newbury Park, CA: Sage.

Boyer, E. L. (1990). *Scholarship reconsidered: Priorities of the professoriate.* Princeton, NJ: Princeton University.

Butler, J. E., & Walter, J. C. (Eds.). (1991). *Transforming the curriculum: Ethnic studies and women's studies.* New York: State University of New York Press.

Byard, P. J. (1981). Quantitative genetics of human skin color. *Yearbook of Physical Anthropology, 24*, 123-137.

Carmichael, S., & Hamilton, C. V. (1967). *Black power: The politics of liberation in America.* New York: Vintage.

Cortes, C. (1991). Pluribus & unum: The quest for community amid diversity. *Change, 23*(5), 8-15.

Daniels, L. A. (1991). Diversity, correctness, and campus life: A closer look. *Change, 23*(5), 16-24.

D'Emilio, J., & Freedman, E. (1988). *Intimate matters: A history of sexuality in America.* New York: Harper & Row.

Dennis, R. (1981). Socialization and racism: The white experience. In B. P. Bowser & R. Hunt (Eds.), *Impacts of racism on white Americans* (pp. 71-86). Beverly Hills, CA: Sage.

Dewart, J. (Ed.). (1991). *The state of black America, 1991.* New York: National Urban League.

Drake, St. C. (1990). *Black folk here and there* (2 vols.). Los Angeles: UCLA Center for African-American Studies.

Elder, J. (1978). Levels of consciousness: Racism and sexism. In N. Schniedewind (Ed.), *Confronting racism and sexism: A practical handbook for educators* (pp. 152-153). New Paltz, NY: Common Ground.

Ellison, R. (1989). *Invisible man.* New York: Vintage.

Essed, P. (1991). *Understanding everyday racism: An interdisciplinary theory.* Newbury Park: Sage.

Feagin, J. R. (1989). *Racial and ethnic relations.* Englewood Cliffs, NJ: Prentice-Hall.

Feagin, J. R. (1992). The continuing significance of racism and discrimination against black students in white colleges. *Journal of Black Studies, 22*, 546-578.

Festinger, L. (1954). A theory of social comparison processes. *Human Relations, 2*, 117-140.

Freire, P. (1985). *The politics of education: Culture, power and liberation*. South Handley, MA: Bergin & Garvey.

Fuchs, L. H. (1990). *The American kaleidoscope: Race, ethnicity and the civic culture*. Middletown, CT: Wesleyan University Press.

Gates, H. L. (1987, Fall). Authority, (white) power and the (black) critic: It's all Greek to me. *Cultural Critique*, pp. 19-46.

Graves, J. L., Jr. (in press). *Evolutionary biology and human variation: Biological determinism and the mythology of race*. Newbury Park, CA: Sage.

Gudykunst, W. B., & Kim, Y. Y. (1992). *Communicating with strangers: An approach to intercultural communication*. New York: McGraw-Hill.

Hacker, A. (1992). *Two nations: Black and white, separate, hostile, unequal*. New York: Scribner.

Harding, V. (1981). Toward a darkly radiant vision of America's truth: A letter of concern, an invitation to recreation. In C. Reynolds & R. Norman (Eds.), *Community in America: The challenge of habits of the heart* (pp. 67-83). Berkeley: University of California Press.

Harrington, W. (1992). *Crossings: A white man's journal into black America*. New York: Harper-Collins.

Hildalgo, N. M., McDowell, C. L., & Siddle, E. V. (Eds.). (1990). *Facing racism in education* (Vol. 21 of reprint series). Cambridge, MA: Harvard Educational Review.

Jaynes, G., & Williams, R., Jr. (1989). *A common destiny: Blacks and American society*. Washington, DC: National Research Council.

Jones, J. (1972). *Prejudice and racism*. Reading, MA: Addison-Wesley.

Jordan, W. (1968). *White over black: American attitudes toward the negro, 1550-1812*. Chapel Hill: University of North Carolina Press.

Katz, J. (1991). White faculty struggling with the effects of racism. In P. G. Altback & K. Lomotey (Eds.), *Racial crisis in American higher education* (pp. 187-196). Albany: State University of New York Press.

King, J. E. (1990). Dysconscious racism: Ideology, identity, and the miseducation of teachers. *Journal of Negro Education, 60*(2), 133-146.

Kitano, H. (1985). *Race relations*. Englewood Cliffs, NJ: Prentice-Hall.

Ladson-Billings, G. (1991). Beyond multicultural illiteracy. *Journal of Negro Education, 60*(2), 147-157.

Lawrence, C. (1986). The id, the ego, and equal protection: Reckoning with unconscious racism. *Stanford Law Review, 38*, 317-388.

Levine, A., & Cureton, J. (1992). The quiet revolution: Eleven facts about multiculturalism and the curriculum. *Change, 24*, 1.

Lukens, J. (1978). Ethnocentric speech. *Ethnic Groups, 2*, 35-53.

Lurie, T. (1992, Winter). *What it means to be a hyphenated American*. Ford Foundation Report, pp. 16-19.

Minnich, E. K. (1990). *Transforming knowledge*. Philadelphia: Temple University Press.

Nei, M., & Roychoudhury, A. K. (1982). Genetic relationship and evolution of human races. *Evolutionary Biology, 14*, 1-59.

Paige-Pointer, B., & Auletta, G. S. (1990). Restructuring the curriculum: Barriers and bridges. *Women Studies Quarterly, 17*(1/2), 86-94.

Peck, M. S. (1978). *The road less traveled.* New York: Touchstone.

Pinderhughes, E. (1989). *Understanding race, ethnicity and power.* New York: Free Press.

Pinkney, A. (1976). *Red, black, and green: Black nationalism in the United States.* Cambridge, UK: Cambridge University Press.

Pinkney, A. (1984). *The myth of black progress.* Cambridge, UK: Cambridge University Press.

Rose, M. (1989). *Lives on the boundary: The struggles and achievements of America's underprepared.* New York: Free Press.

Rosovsky, H. (1990). *The university: An owner's manual.* New York: Norton.

Rothenberg, P. S. (1988). *Racism and sexism: An integrated study.* New York: St. Martin's.

Simonson, R., & Walker, S. W. (Eds.). (1988). *The gray wolf annual five: Multicultural literacy.* St. Paul, MN: Graywolf.

Snowden, F. (1970). *Blacks in antiquity: Ethiopians in the Greco-Roman experience.* Cambridge, UK: Belknap.

Sollars, W. (1986). *Beyond ethnicity: Consent and descent in American culture.* New York: Oxford University Press.

Stewart, J. (1990). Introduction from the editor and to the assumptions behind this book. In J. Stewart (Ed.), *Bridges, not walls* (pp. 2-10). New York: McGraw-Hill.

Stringer, C. B., & Andrews, P. (1988). Genetic and fossil evidence for the origin of modern humans. *Science, 239,* 1263-1269.

Takaki, R. (1990). *Iron cages: Race and culture in 19th-century America.* New York: Oxford University Press.

Taylor, C. (1992). *Multiculturalism and the politics of recognition.* Princeton, NJ: Princeton University Press.

Terkel, S. (1992). *Race: How blacks and whites think and feel about the American obsession.* New York: New Press.

Trungpa, C. (1988). *Shambhala: The sacred path of the warrior.* Boston: Shambhala.

Van Dijk, T. (1987). *Communicating racism: Ethnic prejudice in thought and talk.* Newbury Park, CA: Sage.

Van Sertima, I. (Ed.). (1988). *African presence in early Europe.* New Brunswick, NJ: Transaction Books.

Watts, R. J., & Carter, R. T. (1991). Psychological aspects of racism in organizations. *Group and Organizational Studies, 16,* 328-344.

Watzlawick, P., Beavin, J. H., & Jackson, D. D. (1967). *The pragmatics of human communication.* New York: Random House.

Wideman, J. E. (1984). *My brother's keeper.* New York: Holt, Rinehart & Winston.

Williams, C. (1992). *No place to hide.* San Francisco: Harper.

Wilmot, W. W. (1987). *Dyadic communication.* New York: Random House.

Wilson, W. J. (1988, May/June). The ghetto underclass and the social transformation of the inner city. *The Black Scholar,* pp. 10-17.

About the Authors

Benjamin P. Bowser is Associate Professor of Sociology and Social Services at California State University (CSU) at Hayward and a board member of the Center for the Student of Intercultural Relations. He is Associate Editor of Sage Race Relations Abstracts (London), has published, received grants, and consulted in race relations, management, and AIDS prevention. He is a 1992-1993 Field Faculty Fellow of the California Field Poll Institute. He has held administrative positions at Cornell and Stanford universities and directed programs at Santa Clara University and the Western Interstate Commission for Higher Education.

Gale S. Auletta is Professor of Communication and Co-Director of the Center for the Study of Intercultural Relations at CSU Hayward. She publishes, receives grants, and consults in the areas of intercultural communication and integrating multicultural perspectives into higher education. She is corecipient of the Woman of the Year Award for contributing to diversity in the CSU, 1988.

Terry Jones is Professor of Sociology and Social Services, Vice-President of the California Faculty Association, and Co-Director of the Center for the Study of Intercultural Relations at CSU Hayward. He publishes, receives grants, and consults in the areas of race and racism, criminal justice, and the sociology of sports. He is the recipient of the Human Rights Award for California Faculty Association, 1991, and was voted Outstanding Professor, 1990.

In 1985, Gale Auletta and Terry Jones founded the Center for the Study of Intercultural Relations (CSIR). The CSIR staff gathers and conducts research, generates and promotes multicultural curriculum and training models for the classroom and corporations, and conducts workshops and provides consulting services for corporations and nonprofits.